5 2 PROV

DEPRESSIC ....TAUMA

Irish Holistic Wisdom

Fiann Ó Nualláin

MERCIER PRESS

MERCIER PRESS

Cork

www.mercierpress.ie

ISBN: 978-1-78117-861-4

eBook: 978-1-78117-830-0

Cover design: Sarah O'Flaherty

Printed and bound in the EU.

CONTENTS

ACKNOWLEDGEMENTS

Some books can be a lifetime in the making, or more to the point a lifetime lived to get to the page, and in that long journey there are of course countless encounters with inspirational and sharing people, whom by their gifts and gift, motivate or direct one on to better understanding or a better quality of life lived thereafter, *buíochais* agus *beannachtaí* to those good souls. Some whose names I did not catch, some shy of a mention, some mentioned in other books and places, some in the bibliography here. I pass this book on with the same good will and humanity you previously gave to me.

On the technical side – a *buíochas* to Siobhán McNamara for an ear to my Irish agus *buíochas* to the team at Mercier press for their longstanding support of my work and their skills of taking a manuscript into book form and on into the wider world.

INTRODUCTION

Resilience is not just the capacity to endure setback or trauma, or carry the toll of it, it is the ability to move forward with your life post-crisis, to live a life after the event, without the event continuing to impinge on your day to day. Resilience is the capacity to encounter challenging situations as challenges and not as catastrophes. Resilience is problem solving and problem resolving. Resilience is not letting adversity define you or worse devastate you. The aim of this book is to hone resilient traits or acquire a renewed resilient mind-set – resilience is an inherent human trait after all, we stumble our way into walking, we babble our way into talking, we learn from failures and setbacks, we thrive on adaptability, we continue to the next challenge or learning/achieving opportunity. Our life experiences and ongoing depressive episodes may have made us lose connection with that part of ourselves but the 52 proverbs of this book and the exercises that accompany them, aim to make that connection again. The challenge-orientated asks of the exercises forge a challenge-orientated perception of issues affecting our emotional sense of self, and so the realisation that something can be done. It is not game over; it is game afoot. We can overcome, we need not be so affected.

Feeling down is a natural human experience; we all encounter it from time to time. A disappointment in one's life plans; upsetting news; the experience of a bereavement or the loss/collapse of a friendship, relationship or job; or even of a held worldview or moral standpoint, a reaction to world events, the ongoing complications of one's personal life, a dip in good circumstances or a decrease in one's sense of wellbeing or achievement potential can all trigger sadness and a demotivation.

Sometimes 'the down' can persist long enough or spiral deep enough, to develop into a clinical depression. For most 'the downs' come and go as bumps, potholes or the twists and turns on the life's highway – not pleasant but negotiable, or good riddance in the rear-view mirror. To others the accumulation of such swerves and prangs or the constant burn-up of reserves to try to navigate around, seem to completely complicate or grind down any movement forward. We get stuck. The idea of this book is a needed push or tow, some necessary repairs and a refilled tank, but also a better road map, if not even a better road ahead.

Depression, which is characterised as a persistent sadness or continued emotional deflation combined with a lack of interest or enjoyment from previously rewarding or enjoyable activities can be overwhelming or all-consuming. Its presence in one's life can affect one's ability to function, participate or indeed act in one's own self-interest. Help is required to get back one's purpose, energy and mindset to live a rewarding life. With the help of this book, but also via one's GP, counselling services and community supports, it is highly treatable.

On an evolutionary note, if pain is an evolutionary adaption to stop further damage to the affected area and so take care, and anxiety is an evolutionary trait to avoid danger or risky behaviour and so survive then the evolutionary biology of depression may just be as something to shield one from overload, to slow the brain and body until circumstances abate. My own depression often took on this hedgehog curl when the world got too much for me – my depression while wounding and distressful (in the raw and in the numb manifestations) encased me in my world away from the bigger threats. Ok it is more complex than that and sometimes you can get pierced by your own spikes and even stay in the curled ball longer than is needed but I learned to take my depression as time outs, as time outs to work out the problem, as time to figure other ways of self-care and response than perfecting the curl up strategy.

Evolutionary biologist believe that the analytical rumination of depression is this adaptation of the brain to keep one focused on complex interpersonal problems until one can arrive at a resolution or in the case of a situational stimuli (occasioned period of transition, upset or grief) until a spontaneous remission occurs. The good of that is that's not a broken brain, that's a self-protecting brain. That's a brain which seeks to work in our favour. The saying 'its ok to not be ok' takes on some extra rational. Of course, I also say let's advocate 'it's even better to get better'. If we can control the rumination, solve some of the issues, avoid the glitches of a negative bias, then we can build back stronger. Get to the other side, better.

Other evolutionary theories include the expression of depression as the facilitation of attachment within the family/tribe, encouraging bonding or care toward the wounded, helping reducing risk of social exclusion. Some have proffered it as a means to disengage from unobtainable goals or withdraw from an overwhelming circumstance, to buffer while changes or time-led resolution is required and even to warding off attack following loss of status. And we can see those things in the once temporary deference that can become deeper rooted self-deprivation, or the withdrawal/conservation of energies in episodes becoming a negative worldview and conditioned response. The good of it, complicated in making it worse. But we can unpick that too. Rewire better responses. Evolve a different strategy.

Depression is a common mental health disorder manifesting as low mood, lethargy and poor concentration. There is often the experience of repetitive negative thought patterns, a sense of lower self-esteem, feelings of emptiness or a rawness to emotional disturbance which can compound the depression or set up the vicious cycle effect – causing one to seek to withdraw from people, places and daily activities. Depression can also be complicated by an array of other psychological issues such as guilt, self-depreciation, pessimism. It often elicits disturbed sleep and appetite, reduced libido, irritability, increased pain sensitivity and a range of physical discomforts.

The underlying causes of depression can be complex, with interactions between social/societal, psychological and biological factors all at play. Genetics and environment can also influence its development. Life events such as childhood adversity and adult trauma can be at the heart of the issue. It can often be a matter of chemistry, the disruption in hormones and the emotional impact of pregnancy and post birth responsibility/reality in postnatal depression or the insufficient serotonin levels that come with seasonal effective disorder.

The fact is, our thoughts and our feelings, our emotional realm, is reactive and interlinked, it can be stimulated by events and moments, by how we experience ongoing life. We can be programmed by what has gone before, by our past upsets and traumas. The trick is to unpick those problems not pick at them and to let those wounds heal, to find the solutions to avoiding future wounds; to find a way to not let both our natural inbuilt negative bias (needed for survival) and the intensified negative bias and conclusions of our lived experience with depression (our conditioned response) to halt a way of having and experiencing a good, full and productive, happier life.

Of course, this book is not about the search for happiness – the search for happiness is not necessarily the antidote to depression, in fact that search may be a psychological complication we don't need. No, this book is about a more effective remedy to the malady. It is about stopping the search for unhappiness. We may find more good along the way, even hunt some out, which is part of building a resilience and a positive bias. But the pursuit is in participating less with the negative, uncurling and stepping into a wider world with confidence and a broader skillset.

This whole book is about reframing your reactions and responses to both actual negative experiences and to perceived ones. It is about overcoming being overwhelmed by habitual emotions and physical symptoms, or indeed by the lack of feeling that can accompany depression. It is about resetting how to discern between a disappointment and a catastrophe, between a thought and a consequential feeling, between a bad day and 'nothing goes right for me'.

It is about how to wind back, disarm and decommission any such patterns of negative thinking or conditioned mind-set. To escape the negative bias and find more positives. It uses the scientifically validated methods of cognitive behavioural psychology and the helpful practices of mindfulness and positive psychology to build a resilience and an array of circuit breakers to halt dark thinking and depressive episodes in their tracks. It is about moving forward with more than hope, with the skills to cope and the ability to redirect.

And yes, whatever you are sad, depressed or down about right now is genuine and real to you, is affecting your quality of life right now but what if you could make it less? Less deep, less frequent, less impacting. What if you could see and perceive it differently? What if you could refocus on not potentially what will go wrong, what has gone south, what past injury is on today's agenda but on what bright thing might be on the horizon, what might be on the up, what might be the good to be had. Enough of pondering and ruminating the bad outcome possibilities, sure they are only possibilities you play over, not certainties. What if the only potential at the table was your full potential – your capacity to live the fullest life, unburdened from obstacles to happiness, contentment and even achievements? What if you could dismantle any acquired negative bias and construct a new positive pre-disposition. What if you could be in a good place? What if you could be the you that you want to be?

To that end this book takes a holistic approach. One of treating the whole person – not just the emotional self, but the social, the creative and the spiritual self – your full self. I have been a holistic practitioner for many years and in my therapeutic work I not only seek to solve the pressing problem, but look to the entire lived experience and circumstances of the client. To move out of the shadow of self-doubt, depression, trauma, anxiety into the sunshine of living a good life. 'Good' is not a moral judgment here, it the full blossoming of a positive and experiential life, one worth seeking and filled with rewards and opportunities – one not stilted by the clouds of apprehension or misery.

So throughout this book there will be prompts to get creative, to go intermingle, to dance, to do some yoga, to hug a tree or bang a gong. I also find the use and experience of alternative therapies to be a helpful liberation from woes and worries, to be of proven remedial benefit but also to further circuit-break current emotional and physiological manifestation. To get a feel-good factor in one's life more frequently than a feel-down factor. So yes, the impetus invoked throughout is to go experience the good (positive) and not feel bad (negative).

The 'holistic' in the title is my way to consider the totality of the person, not to see them as their symptoms, rather to build resilience to the problems they face and to encourage a mind-set of positivity to all our worldview, world experience, greater good of life, to a life well lived, and yes, it is ok to hang a dream catcher, its ok to dream big. Your life does not have to remain the current nightmare it may be. The strategies of this book are to open up a brighter life as well as shutting down the triggers of sadness, regret and depression.

Depression as a negative emotional experience, as a stress response, as a psychological phase, has indeed a spectrum basis; a sliding scale of intensity and frequency. So no matter what end of the scale or how it manifests in you, the techniques in this book help to circuit-break the experience and retrain the brain out of episodes. One may need to stick with the medication or the medical supervision a bit longer but the aim here is to build strategies to overcome what brings you down. There are supports beyond this book, it doesn't all have to be on you alone. Helplines, apps, support groups, drop-in centres, social prescribing via your GP, community based, HSE and private counselling services, and various charities and associations that can assist your journey forward.

Prolonged or repeated experience of depression may tip us into avoidance of places, people or situations, may crush our ambitions and hopes, may alter how we perceive ourself and indeed put a persistent negative gloom over our world-view. The concepts in this book seek to reverse that path and navigate a more positive route into well-being and control over your emotions, thoughts and experience of life. It sets out to help you make the changes necessary.

There is the proverb that states *change is the breath of life*. Change is the energy to transform. Change is the energy behind catching your breath and finding a way towards a healthy and unhindered life. We can get our life back; we can infuse it with positivity and pleasant outcomes. We can make changes. We are not condemned to eternal gloom and doom. There is more to life.

Throughout I utilise mindfulness, cognitive behavioural therapeutics and positive psychology to boost our capacity to take back control, to have coping mechanisms and to diminish the grip of gloom. The aim of this book is not to just be a coping strategy but to be a genuine path to a fuller life beyond depression and negative thinking. And while each proverb, and the exercises or actions connected to each, are steps to overcome rumination, worrisome thoughts, sad and numb cycles and being stuck in a perception of perpetual negativity, they are also pathways to living that fuller life – to engage with your true self, your full potential capacity, with a prosocial self, with a self positively connected to nature and the world around you. To the whole you, with all your full potential in the positive.

My aim is not only to dial that negative bias back, but also to bring vigilance and a stronger register to the good going on – to engineer a positivity bias. The actions and exercise are designed to strengthen an awareness of positivity and to work with constructive motivations and our natural neuroplasticity to rebuild the brain circuitry and chemistry in favour of a positive bias – of a more frequent experience of the good things.

We programme ourselves with the words we tell ourselves – just consider for a moment how much of your sadness or deflatedness is self-talk – the inner critic or the echoes of detractors or previous perpetrators, the playback of former incidents, the repeat, repeat, repeat and thus repeated dejection and despondency. So, the words in this book are a way to programme a different approach to life. In part, it is about reframing and altering our narrative from all the bad to all the good, but it is also a way to prime the brain for acceptance of the good. It is written with neurolinguistic programming in mind, so repetition of words or phrases and word selection are ways of reinforcing the message, ways of helping the mind pick up on the point. You may find similar patterns in guided meditation or in well-being apps – all designed to make it easy to put into practice the solutions they offer.

Our depression has wired our brain, personality and the way we experience living, but we can rewire it to a better state of operations. We can make little changes that have a big long-term impact. We are not talking 'back to factory settings' we are talking 'upgrade'.

I have used these techniques in my life to overcome the hyper-vigilance, worry and depression, present from childhood – a combination of some childhood adversity and the manifestations of intergenerational trauma in a sphere of influence around me, compounded by my own personal seasonal affected disorder. Over the years, I had, by my reactions to experiences, trained myself to deepen a negative bias and sorrowful outlook, it stilted my life, made friendships and relationships difficult to sustain and while I could mask it long enough to get through a working day, there really were few days that were not hard work.

I had not yet come across the *seanfhocal*/proverb – *it won't always be raining* or indeed *sunshine follows gloom*. All I could see was the rain or the raincloud forming. I was looking at the momentary experiences of calm or peace or contentment as the transitory part, I wasn't seeing that the pain, the hurt, the darkness, were also transitory. I wasn't maximising the dry and unthreatening days and I was stuck in bad weather. It took me a long time to see it, to change my reactions and responses – to get out from under the cloud. It took some perseverance after the initial insight, but I had always loved the poetics and humour in proverbs and began using them as circuit breakers, affirmations and ancestral advice. I found support, solace and strategy there.

For many years now, I have chosen to live each day to the best of my ability, not frozen by past or future, not halted by self-recrimination or picking at old wounds, not anticipating the next slight or hurt, not waiting for the next darkness to descend. Situations and triggers can sometimes still arise, but I can let them go, I don't need to grab on anymore. Of course, there is always the possibility that an unforeseen storm could come and knock me over, but now I know I don't have to stay down, I am not scanning for it to the neglect of enjoying calm days, now instead, I am ready to predict the sunshine to come.

I look at it now believing there is a world out there to explore, a life to be lived and the weather just dictates my footwear not my mind-set. I don't self-identify as a psychological disturbance, I find myself in life, in living more mindfully and fully. This is not a book about the history of my troubles, yet my own pathway out has informed it. I may reference some of my experiences within certain passages, but they are universal experiences and while we are all unique and psychological complications come in different forms, strengths and durations – there are some universal wisdoms to help get through and beyond such experiences.

The contents here are based both upon first-hand experience and the culmination of years of participation with mindfulness and psychotherapies. This is how I mastered and diminished my own personal demons and how I have helped others commence their path to vanquish theirs.

In the useful tools section and peppered throughout the book, there are skill sets to assist that different way. Some you will really enjoy and even relish and for some people there may be a few that are slightly embarrassing or awkward and others that may even be terrifying – but hold strong and conquer. Remember the stoic poet Ovid, *Perfer et obdura, dolor hic tibi proderit olim – Be patient and tough; someday all this pain will be useful to you.* You might want to write that down and stick it on the fridge. Do the same with any of the proverbs here that really resonate with you.

Think of these proverbs as the advice our ancestors wished to pass on, a far-reaching chain of respect and self-care, a goldmine of hard learned experience, a loving kindness to the next generation. Think of these proverbs as more than ancient sense but as contemporary affirmations. Affirmations are not fool's errands, they are the stories we tell ourselves, so instead of telling ourselves how hard it is to be ourselves with all that baggage that we lug around, let's write a new narrative and navigate our world with a brighter more successful outlook. Let's look beyond the clouds, they are breaking anyway, the sun is cutting several shafts through, soon it will be all blue skies and serotonin release. It is never always raining; sunshine always follow gloom.

PROVERBIAL WISDOM

Proverbs are often thought of as clever idioms or witty observations, but in truth they are the encoded wisdom of our ancestors, incorporating the keenest insights and best life advice stretching back through the ages. They have been distilled over generations, passed on like life-coaching batons from generation to generation. Embodying not just the cultural attitudes of the place they originate in but the survival advice and moral codes that each generation wishes the next generation to cherish and learn from. Proverbs are generated and known in all cultures, worldwide. They are perhaps the oldest teaching tools, the most effective transmission of how to live a life well and are invaluable as road maps through the vicissitudes of life.

So, the proverbs in this book are the insightful nuggets of the collective consciousness, experience and of the tried and tested. The proverb or *seanfhocal* (old word) alone is a potent expression of a mind-set, the Irish proverbs selected here are standard bearers of a way of thinking that has brought resilience, overcoming, solace and positive motivation to each generation. The Irish wisdom of ancient heritage is so pertinent today.

And while each *seanfhocal*/proverb offers a psychological insight, perception shift or attitude adjustment, the exercises that accompany them are designed to reinforce the proverbial wisdom, to sink it in by way of a practice, task or additional learning aid. By getting you to perform or consider other options, it is not solely a reframing of current woes but a gaining of skills to work through the vicissitudes of life and tackle the dynamics of depression.

The idea is to incorporate into your life, those concepts and tools contained within this book that strike a chord with you personally – they are the ones that will especially work for you as they come to fill your days with meaning as well as a method out of pain. The book is laid out as a programme where you can take a proverb each week, over a year and take the time to develop the skills and engage with the exercises, building each week, strengths and strategies to developing a more resilient and focused mind-set, to undermine the grips of sadness or the periods of numbness and free yourself from triggers and pitfalls. Of course, you can read it all at your own pace, in one sitting, over a few days or as a dip in dip out and still benefit from the proverbial wisdom and the insights and revelations they prompt and provoke. As you read these profound ancient words and follow the exercises, a pathway to a more in control, full potential self will become clear.

USEFUL TOOLS

Every good worker knows that good tools make for an easier job; be that a sharp axe or a smart phone or a well-oiled machine. The work that you want to do on yourself also requires tools (or skill sets) that will make the job easier to accomplish. There is an old Irish proverb pertinent here; *Sí leith na ceirde an úirleais – The tools are half the trade,* it stresses the importance of good tools or quality skills in accomplishing the task – they are half of what is required. Will power, brute force, perspiration, passion, desire, diligence, enthusiasm or even desperation won't get you there alone – tools are a prerequisite.

In Ireland, phrases such as 'half the battle', 'half the job' or 'half the trade' are employed to express that your endeavourers are being sped up – helped along and assisted by something – that doing the thing or having the item in hand, is getting you there faster and more completely. A kettle is half the battle in making a cup of tea, breath control is half the battle in attaining meditative states, and a journal may be half the battle in identifying the triggers of your sorrows.

It is interesting to note that many of the *seanfhocail,* can have an extra nuance, can reveal a second truth – this one also reminds us that acquiring the tools is only half the trade, using them is the other half. It's not worth a fig if you know how to relax but never relax. It's no benefit mentally understanding how to do several yoga asanas but never physically performing them. Knowing that you need to make changes is not making changes. Wanting to be free of repetitive thoughts or self-damaging behaviours is not doing enough of the job. Get the appropriate tool to do the job.

Here follows a brief introduction to some of the tools pertinent to the job of creating a more positive self, of living a more mindful and grounded life, of taking control of your emotional well-being, of building resilience and equanimity, and of enjoying the joys of life too.

Mindfulness

Mindfulness at its core is a spiritual tool – best known in the Buddhist tradition as Sati and a key practice on the path to enlightenment. Its essence being that by entering a state of 'attentive awareness' – that's being fully present to the moment-to-moment reality of the present, observing without judgement, being without biases – is a way of coming fully alive to the reality of things. This practise of being of original mind or what some frame as being in 'the now of the now', is the switching on of your spirit, the manifesting of your pure reality – it is your alive essence unhindered by ego and emotions – the you without layers of conditioning; one might even say 'the natural you' or 'the enlightened self'.

The Buddhist spiritual discourses on establishing sati/ mindfulness can be found in the Satipaṭṭhāna Sutta and the Mahāsatipaṭṭhāna Sutta, where it is also highlighted that the intent of the Buddha was to see mindfulness as a means of 'the purification of beings, for the overcoming of sorrow and lamentation, for the extinguishing of suffering and grief, for walking on the path of truth, for the realisation of nirvana'. And while each of those objectives is a spiritual motivation, one can't but notice a psychological function in 'overcoming sorrow and lamentation'.

In recent decades, the popularity of contemporary mindfulness, which some like to call secular mindfulness, is considered a form of the practice utilised to achieve equanimity and control over stress and the strains of modern life – as a tool of destressing and finding inner peace. But it can be much more than a relaxation programme – all the mindful techniques continue to have application as both a path to enlightenment and to extinguishing suffering and grief. Embraced now as a tool by western psychology, mindful practices are utilised to treat anxiety, obsessive compulsive disorders, depression, and other disturbances in mental well-being – with great success.

That accomplishment is because mindful practices bring one to a reality that is not clouded by thought biases or emotionally-triggered judgments or preconceptions, it allows your psychological self to experience the world or situation (and your part in it) for what it really is. As a psychological tool, mindfulness meditation and practices are seen to liberate yourself from the clutter of dissonant thoughts and manage better those pings, pangs and stings of life's vicissitudes. It is not just attaining a peace of mind but attaining neuroplasticity – retraining how the signalling brain reacts, bringing more self-control. Being in the now – right here, right now, awake and present – there is neither time nor place for catastrophising or becoming overwhelmed.

Mindfulness is a way of being more responsive and less reactive, it is a way to have better clarity with thoughts arising or moving through and discerning which emotions to pay attention to and which to let go. You can acknowledge the thought and even its emotion, but you don't have to grasp at it, or invest the rest of your day in it. That anxious moment, that depressive trigger, that inner critic, they can all pass like clouds. Mindfulness is a means of control. You control your breath, you control your thoughts, you control your emotions, you control your reality. This won't halt every bad situation or complicated circumstance, but it will give you control over how you are in the face of those circumstances. It will strengthen your resolve and your resilience, but it will also increase your participation and enjoyment with life. It will, over time, manifest a stronger frequency of better situations and achieve more positive outcomes. Here are some of its techniques/practices:

Conscious awareness: This is both the goal of mindfulness and the way to attain mindfulness. Conscious awareness is simply being present in the moment, being present to each moment, moment by moment. It is experiencing reality and yourself with clarity and without judgement, obstacles or disturbance.

You do it by simply becoming aware of what is happening, or what you are doing, right now in the moment it is occurring. It is being alert and awake to the moment, not daydreaming, fearing, ruminating, or fantasising through it. It is simply meeting the moment with your full self, meeting it mindfully (consciously) not with a mind full (self-consciously or half distracted).

It takes practice to develop this ability and there are several practices that hone the skill; following your breath, engaging your senses, and mindfulness meditations including the techniques described later in this book, such as body scans and progressive muscle relaxation and then there are mindful virtues – such as loving kindness and gratitude – peppered through this book.

You can think of mindfulness/conscious awareness as a lifestyle, as a personality trait, as a spiritual dimension or even as a psychological coping strategy but deliberately living a more mindful life, when and where you can, will enrich your life. The more we do it the more we become it, soon enough mindfulness will be incorporated into your life daily – it will become your way to a better life – and that's not as difficult a task or ask as you might think.

Conscious living: In the context of your current psychological woes, stepping into conscious living is stepping out of striving and struggling with your torment. It can be a circuit breaker to your angst; that moment of truly smelling a flower, or truly tasting a cherry or truly hearing a bird song can transport you to a better place. That mindful moment can bring you to a better frame of mind, but it doesn't only have to be an escape hatch, it can be your more frequent experience of life. You just need to start experiencing life more mindfully.

You can be conscious to breathing, to walking, to sitting to relax or sitting to meditate. Being conscious of your lived moments and the sensations attending, brings you into life, into a purer experience of your life. You can hone this skill to maximise your quality of life; you could consciously eat your favourite meal, or consciously swim in the sea, consciously sit under a tree, consciously make love. You are not seeking enhanced pleasures or desperately trying to find more happiness and less pain – but both come to varying degrees with it – you are just looking to live consciously and not sleepwalk through, or be a puppet in, your own life. That is control, power, and a way of being the force of your own life.

Breath awareness: One of the first steps to mastering conscious awareness is mastering breath control which is really a way to gain control over your attention. It is as much thought control as it is a breathing technique. The breathing technique does occasion a relaxation response and it can be utilised to trigger composure in a troubling situation. The following of the breath also helps to frame a steadier self and more equanimous mind-set as it teaches the brain to be less reactive to experiences and thoughts, and over time builds a neural pathway to reinforce the self-control. It is often employed as the on switch to other mindfulness practices. It is a simple process but may take a time to perfect and the fact that you may have to work at it, is simply building the muscle memory until it's so automatic that you are just in the zone whenever you need.

To attain a conscious awareness of breathing is to simply follow it, let your attention experience it. It is not a chore; it is a skill; it is a discipline. Practice makes perfect. Become consciously aware of your breathing pattern/rhythm – you don't have to slow it or alter it – just noticing the inhale and being with the exhale brings your focus to the process of breathing and not off on a journey of white water rafting your thoughts and emotions. Simply breathe as normal, follow the inhale in, follow the exhale out, be with the next inhale, be with the next exhale and on.

You may get a few breaths followed before your mind starts to drift, that's ok, when you realise you are not breathing in but thinking about household insurance or what's for dinner or that twist in last night's soap opera, then you can just come back to the breath and take a time out from those meandering thoughts. We are not looking to actively suppress thoughts; we can notice them arise and let them pass by without having to latch on and follow them all day. Honing in on your breathing helps the mind stay calm while sharpening your power of concentration, thus enabling you to place your attention where you want it – and that includes *off* repetitive thinking or away from that inner critic.

Simply observe and experience the in and out, in and out, in and out. Each one a physical and psychological repetition – just like gym reps – you are strengthening here. You are not just experiencing respiration you are, by returning from thoughts to breathing, repeatedly, training your brain to focus better on the task in hand not the emotions in the head or gut. Breath awareness can become the switch to your 'in control' self.

Breath awareness is often practised as a meditation, but it can be done standing, walking, waiting for a bus, sitting on a train, cycling, hanging out washing, etc. It is not a dangerous process, it does not hypnotise you, you won't steer the bicycle off the cycle track, miss the bus or drop the baby. It is just breathing, but mindfully – that's aware, not drowsy. Because some people only know on as active and off as unconscious, they find that slowing down makes them sleepy, but it will help you become more focused, more energised, more dynamic. Use it when you want it. Later you can use it when you need it most.

Coming to your senses: The breath exercises are so vital they are primal, they hack into our very life essence and tap into the breath of life to alter our life. There are many different versions, from the simple follow and return, to alternations in rhythm and depth of breath, to alternate nostril breathing, diaphragm breathing and many yogic techniques that can also benefit from appropriation into mindful meditations – but they all use a fundamental necessity of the system – the inhale and exhale of life – to provide a systemic overhaul.

We can follow on from that by reinforcing mindfulness though our senses. If breath is life, the senses are how we navigate life – they evolved to help us perceive our environment and survive in it. They register reality and relay messages to the brain. We use them to read the room every day, we can use them to rearrange the furniture too – we can Feng shui a better mind, organise a more resilient behavioural pattern and fashion our experience of life to happier and higher frequencies more frequently.

In mindfulness, you can use your senses to connect physically to the moment; right now, in this moment, is your skin warm or cold, is there fragrance, sounds? Can you feel the weight of the book or the light from the screen? All that extra awareness of the stimuli around you, fires up the brain, opens the channels, and allows it be imprinted with the good intention or the positivity programme. The senses not only make the moment more real; they make our mind and attention more honed to the message. If in that moment we signal mindfulness or a mindful virtue, then we broadcast that to our very essence.

There are many mindful exercises where the aim is to truly taste something, or to fully hear, touch, smell, see something. The five senses are the anchors to reality and the ladders to entering the now. Perceiving and registering through your senses makes the experience both physical and mental – both external and internal, of the world and of self – it is complete awareness, it is being fully conscious. You notice, recognise or identify through the chosen scene, then observe or experience it without intervening, you meet it, accept it, be with it and live in it for those moments of the experience – that is to be alive to it.

Meditations: Meditation is a good way to practise your mindfulness, to hone the craft and experience of it, to develop a quality of it suitable to bring into the rest of your life. Some people like to reserve their mindfulness for meditation sessions and use that as a weekly or daily respite from strife – that's ok too.

While there are many varieties of meditation, a mindful meditation is one where you are present in it, not lost in the peace or relaxation but awake to the peace or relaxation or whatever the happening is. Traditionally, mindful meditations are ones where you follow your breath, follow a mantra, or pay attention to sensations in your body or grasp the reality of a view or soundscape, it is the return of focus that is the essence and directive of the practice.

You can also engage in some Zen raking, in walking mindfully, in washing the dishes or completing a chore as a dynamic meditation. Not every meditation has to be conducted sitting. There will be several prompts to explore meditation throughout this book and some may not be strict observance meditation in the mindful tradition and more of a visualisation or actively programming nature, but they too can be entered with a mindful approach or as an expression/realisation of a mindful virtue.

A meditation can focus on experiencing, radiation of or receiving of, loving compassion, acceptance or gratitude as much as observation of reality or equanimity in experience. Meditations can be utilised to hone skills as well as to be that daily dose of calm or support.

Mindful virtues: Virtues don't have to be about morality, we can think of them as personal strengths, we can also think of them as tools or assets. There are several mindful virtues such as compassion, gratitude, acceptance that may also be found in Cognitive Behavioural Therapy (CBT), positive psychology and other psychotherapeutic disciplines. These virtues or positive traits can be both a spiritual dynamic and a therapeutic and provide a way to living a fuller life, some are the way to disarm a troubled life: acceptance can replace anger, gratitude can replace regret, loving kindness or self-compassion can replace rumination and anxieties.

Compassion: When it comes to compassion, it is important to understand the motivation/intent. The aim is to practise fellow feeling or concern, not pity. Compassion is not sympathy or even empathy – true compassion is a loving kindness extended without moral superiority or self-reflection. It is not signalling for a hit of do-gooder's endorphins. True compassion is the foundation of humanity that existed even before religion. Compassion is the communication of your soul. It is the manifestation of your resilient and indefeasible spirit in the presence of another, it is recognition of the other and their circumstance. It is solidarity with another soul. It is a moment of oneness.

With depression, anxiety and trauma, the hard part may be in extending compassion towards ourselves. Jack Kornfield, the American spiritual writer and mindfulness advocate, notes, 'if your compassion does not include yourself, it is incomplete'. So self-compassion is also an important component of a mindful life.

Loving-kindness: The Buddhist practice of *metta* aka loving kindness, can be a way of being – an expression of your being, of you being, of your inherent, loving and compassionate self – or it can be a dedicated meditation where you focus or offer benevolent and loving energy toward yourself or others.

There doesn't have to be a song and dance about it. It can be as simple as acknowledgement. In Ireland we say 'hello' as 'Dia Dhuit'; it means 'God to you' – it is not just a hi or a how are you, it is a wish of the grace of God to be upon you, it's a wishing of all that's well in the world to be with you. Perhaps because of that, I love the greeting 'Namaste', which is a small word with a great meaning; it roughly translates from Sanskrit as, 'the divine in me acknowledges the divine in you'. There is nothing more beautiful than to

31

acknowledge another self, to not be all about you, to step beyond current woes and find the love in the world, be the kindness of the world. Through loving kindness, you can recognise the divine in all things and every moment.

You also need to be kind to yourself as well as the rest of the world. With prolonged experiences of angst and depression you may be out of sync with love and kindness to yourself, you may need to reintroduce that energy to yourself before you take it into the world. You can meditate with the focus on your own self, extending positive regard and some loving kindness or from time to time you can simply look in the mirror and greet your own self, 'dia duit' or 'namaste', it's all good.

Acceptance: Successful mindfulness practice is about meeting the true nature of things, it is meeting reality without judgement or trying to intervene or alter – to accept the reality as it is. In learning to accept the present as it is, we also accept ourselves.

Acceptance is the path to equanimity and to self-control – we see the moment for what is – we don't need to cling to our thoughts or pursue ruminations or anxieties. We can let things be, we can let things go, we can move on with our lives. Acceptance is not resigning yourself to your angst or dark moods, it is recognising them for what they are – it is liberating you from their grip.

Gratitude: Saying 'thank you' is often a conditioned response, more about social etiquette and good manners than a genuine heartfelt gratefulness. How often are you present and fully sincere in thankfulness? With depression and anxiety in your life, it can be hard to find things to be thankful for – or at least that's the lie we tell ourselves to stay miserable. There is plenty to be thankful for – even awareness of the pain we are in, because that's the catalyst out of it. Be grateful for the clarity of knowing that you need to change.

Gratitude is also the way to change the situation, it is a circuit breaker, disrupting negative thoughts and experiences with a positive emotional uplift. When we consciously appreciate and acknowledge the good things in life, in a moment, a meditation or journalling exercise, we are stepping out of negative bias and into positive bias, we are tipping the scales in favour of the positive. By acknowledging the good and positive, and being thankful or appreciative of it, we are embracing the acceptance that not all is bad or detrimental.

Gratitude is a way of hunting the good, of harvesting the positive, of feeding the soul.

Cognitive Behavioural Therapeutic (CBT):

Today there is a spectrum of cognitive behavioural therapies, all stemming from the pioneering work of both Albert Ellis whom in the 1950s developed Rational Emotive Behaviour Therapy (REBT), and Aaron T. Beck whom in the 1960s developed cognitive therapy – later, Cognitive Behavioural Therapy (CBT). While there are subtle differences, all are a form of psychotherapeutic treatment that highlights how thoughts and feelings influence behaviour and drive psychosis or troubled episodes; and via a reappraisal of those thoughts and feelings, take constructive steps to realign the self to more beneficial and healthier behaviours.

Cognitive Behavioural Therapies are delivered through one-on-one therapist led sessions where exercises are set to help confront and change any errant/dissonant thinking and to bring about understanding of and control over such thoughts and feelings that can sway one toward distress, depression, anxiety and which foster repeat negative experiences and negative interpretations of your life. CBTs are a way to retrain perception and reactions, to explore a new dynamic of living, to confront what is holding you back and to reveal and enhance what can move you forward and beyond past events and current triggers.

Here I utilise the spirit of CBT and several CBT-style exercises to prompt realisation and change. Mindfulness is often encouraged as a co-therapy to CBT and many aspects overlap; for example, a mindfulness body scan is quite close to a CBT progressive muscle relaxation exercise. Many aspects of positive psychology are also complementary to CBT. We can think our way into negative or detrimental behaviours, but we can also behave or action our way out of trouble into positive thinking. That's the premise of the exercises in this book. It is to not just to cope while you wait for the clouds to pass, it's to ensure you are not so affected by them in the first place.

CBT is about navigating away from dissonant per-ceptions, so too is mindfulness and positive psychology. The interweave of all these approaches throughout this book broadens your toolbox options and speeds the potential to achieve a positive outcome. It will carry you a long way but there is no harm (and all the help) in seeking out a

CBT therapist to continue with the work or in conjunction with your participation with this book as a therapeutic intervention.

Unravelling Cognitive Distortions: CBTs are centred around the idea that how/what we think, how/what we feel and how we act (or react) are interrelated, that one can encourage or provoke the other – that our cognition, our emotion and our behaviour gets fired and wired together. Thinking it's a bad day or I am a bad person can bring up negative emotions that drive how you will respond or act – you may avoid, ruminate or even retaliate.

The aim of CBTs is to find the trigger and question it, to unpick its chain-reaction potential and learn ways to manage or negate its frequency of occurrence. Those triggers are most often labelled as cognitive distortions. CBTs offer a retuning. That is often via the ABC Model, where with a therapist or via therapeutic homework (or in this book through several exercises and actions) one will identify and analyse one's thoughts, feelings and actions, their interactions and their validity as rational or a distorted reaction. The acronym 'ABC', signposts 'A' – for 'Activating Event' (the trigger), 'B' – for 'Belief' (your assumptions to it) and 'C' – for 'Consequences' (the triggered reaction – those negative emotional and behavioural responses).

Activating Event: A neighbour doesn't say hello back as you pass on the street.

Belief: 'I must have offended them' or 'nobody likes me'.

Consequences: You may feel sick to your stomach or start to feel sad/distressed as an emotional consequence. As a behavioural consequence, you may decide to lower your head and not engage today with any other person, you may go home and ruminate.

The CBT exercise is to note the sequence of events then examine your belief; is it a wild assumption, is it grounded in a real fact, what might be an alternative explanation? Explore if the belief is reasonable or distorted. Consider if there is an alternate belief/assumption/perception to be made and how that may lead to a different outcome.

What if they had an ear set in listing to music and didn't hear you. What if they were so caught up in their own thoughts and problems, they just didn't notice you. What if they are just that type of grumpy or unmannerly person to everyone. What if their lack of response has absolutely nothing to do with you at all.

By deconstructing the chain reaction and looking at alternate viewpoints and outcomes one learns to be less judgmental and reactive – and more in control. You can train yourself to drop the negative assumptions so they are triggered less frequently.

Cognitive Restructuring: By becoming aware of over-reactive or flawed assumptions we can opt to encourage more positive interpretations. By becoming aware of these patterns which reinforce the distorted beliefs, we can begin to challenge them and reconstruct a different response to the events and situations we encounter in life. We can think, feel and behave in ways that don't have to equate to psychological distress. The ask of this book is to restructure.

The here and now: One of the key principles of CBT is the focus on the current crisis and to tackle the symptoms/consequences that you are struggling with right now. Sure knowing why you are prone to become depressed or anxious or angry, knowing the pathology of your problem (be it a recent setback such as job loss or bereavement or an old trauma such as parental neglect, bullying, childhood physical or emotional abuse), is a way to grasp its dimensions and build a coherent strategy to disarm it, but in tackling and short-circuiting the sensations of anguish, panic or torment in the moments they arise is to overcome in the here and now, to get beyond the past and find a grounding for the future.

Knowing that the moment of pain, doubt, sorrow or suicide ideation stems from parental neglect, bereavement, bullying, abuse or whatever original trauma, is no salve to the anguish, panic or torment. Discovering how to diminish the anguish, disarm the panic, halt the immediate torment is exceedingly helpful in the moment of occurrence. Yet to build a life beyond anxiety it is important to address those traumas and triggers too when the panic is not the pressing issue.

Exposure and Response Prevention: CBTs regularly guide you to confront your thinking and any associated dissonance but it may also encourage you to visit those painful triggers, to put yourself in front of what normally elicits a negative feeling or behaviour and modify the depth of feeling or the typical reaction. It takes procedure, practice and time, to get to the point where the trigger no longer triggers, and in this book you may be asked to go out of your comfort zone via some actions and exercises; all that is to build a capacity to encounter new and novel experiences and to build a resilience to awkwardness and discomfort.

You won't be asked to juggle twelve rattle snakes and four tarantulas but you might be asked to visualise visiting a snake or spider house in a zoo or to journal about how you feel when you think of a snake or spider. This practice-run of the visiting and 'surviving' the experience, builds muscle memory of having survived, thus diminishing the fear of the next occurrence and building in your mind more positive behavioural responses.

Habit training: Depression and anxiety are habits that you have picked up – certainly if you have a regular tendency to experience one or the other. They are habitual in their frequency but also, in the other connotation of habit – addictive, ingrained – they may become hard to give up. Cognitive behavioural therapies and the other suggestions within this book aim to break negative habits and build positive ones. There is repetition of asks in this book and I encourage you to repeat enjoyable and rewarding tasks, re-engage with what brings you confidence, clarity, peace of mind and fulfilment. Make joy a habit. Make gratitude a habit. Make loving kindness a habit. Make the positive life habitual.

Pleasant Activity Scheduling: A part of making the positive life habitual is to schedule – purposefully plan and carry out – pleasant activates, to indulge the joys of your life over the woes of your life. It is liberating. Replacing the negative with the positive is not only circuit-breaking the negativity, but it is increasing the positivity experienced.

There will be prompts in this book to do so, but why not start later today – fancy a pistachio gelato, a walk in a park, a trip to a museum, a moment of birdsong, a hot date or a hot chocolate or cold beer with a good friend – go make it happen. Accustom yourself to think each day of doing something rewarding and enjoyable, in doing such activities that produce higher levels of positive emotions in your daily life yields a consistency of well-being experiences, a stronger narrative of doing well, an actual positive emotion life.

Journalling: On one level journalling is a technique of 'gathering data' about our emotions, behaviours, and thoughts – to build a picture of our current life and how we react to its highs and lows. It is a way to analyse what we experience and then to modify responses to experiences. It can be a mood diary but one where we can also figure out how to change, adapt, or cope with each significant occurrence and even with some insignificant (but triggering) ones too. It can be a place to do the ABCs, to schedule the pleasant activities, to express loving kindness and gratitude and other virtues.

It doesn't have to be published or shared, it doesn't have to be a detailed memoir, but it can be as creative or as expressive as you wish. It's a workbook, to think about your problems and build solutions. For the moment, it can be a great focus point for your journey towards change, a prompt to action and a record of actions taken. It may be a source of solace as well as information and may become a lifelong pastime.

Positive Psychology

While there are stepping-stones in the work of Abraham Maslow, Erich Fromm and Carl Rogers, Martin Seligman developed Positive Psychology, and several major proponents include Mihaly Csikszentmihalyi and Christopher Peterson, as a new perspective on emotional well-being. While the bulk of psychotherapies are orientated around fixing a problem or identifying the weakness, Positive psychology on the other hand is more about what's going right and identifying your strengths.

It is often framed as the psychology of what makes life most worth living, it could be considered as the 'how to' of making the most of life. There is an emphasis on building cognitive and behavioural patterns of a positive bias and experiencing a better quality of life, a life enriched with not just happier moments but meaning and purpose – to explore and flex your character strengths, to be more in touch with the attributes of courage, hope, gratitude, joyousness, comradery, etc.

The Positive Psychology interventions in this book are not just about dispersing the clouds, they are also about what to do when the sun comes back. They are about year-round, life long, emotional well-being and to be frank, not just swapping positive for negative but replacing floundering with flourishing. There are overlaps with aspects of CBT and mindfulness practices – which assist an effective triangulation of targeted approaches/responses – enriching actions and exercises that help get us into the mode of a productive and rewarding life.

Much of the *modus operandi* and scientific research of

Positive Psychology is based upon the PERMA model proposed by Seligman to explore, focus and strengthen the five facets of well-being. The acronym signposts P – Positive emotional experiences, E – Engagement (participation with life including rewarding activities, positive actions, awe, flow, etc.), R – Relationships and our roles/needs as social creatures, M – Meaning (purpose, validation, direction) and finally A – Accomplishment /Achievement. These five components are the sum of happiness or the formula for a happy and motivated life.

Often the terms positive thinking and positive psychology are used interchangeably, and while positive psychology would incorporate a lot of positive thinking and optimism training, it is much more than willing the good, it is tools to enable the better. It is not blind hope, it is not refusal to see and acknowledge the negative, it is a set of ways to refocus on the positive and disarm the negative realities. Thinking that the shark might have a full belly or extending kind regards to it, is not as good an option as climbing back onto the capsized boat.

Positive psychology is about knowing which is the positive choice. That, like everything else, comes with interaction and integration – practice makes perfect – the more you explore the positive choices and actions, the stronger the muscle memory in times of crisis.

The enriching and proactive nature of positive psychology techniques such as affirmations, finding a different way of looking at a situation, and considering the whole or wider aspects of the current situation, and not just the 'problematic' aspects, all complement problem-focused psychology in therapeutic scenarios and are positive life skills. The spirit and practicalities of positive psychology is interwoven with the exercises throughout this book and in its undertaking to support self-acceptance, autonomy, positive relations, healthy rational, purpose in life and so on.

Many Positive Psychology interventions/exercises mirror those found in CBT and mindfulness – so practices such as gratitude, loving kindness and self-compassion can be seen as a common denominator pathway to moving beyond anxiety, depression and past trauma. In the modern world one might often see a hashtag such as #itsoktonotbeok and yes that breaks the stigma, but the goal really must be to be ok. Positive Psychology is getting to #beingokwithbeingok.

A huge part of Positive Psychology interventions is not just the new narrative potential and how we can learn to see the glass as half full and even enjoy the drinking of it but in how a lot of the Positive psychology is also about practising prosocial skills and activities. This is the way to address self-imposed social isolation that often accompanies or deepens depressive episodes and which can heighten the 'lost' feelings of anxiety and trauma-memory episodes. The prosocial is not just safety in numbers or avoiding being alone, it is how positive human interactions such as sharing, compassion, laughter, conversation, boost perceptions of well-being and even elevates well-being chemistry in our brains and bloodstream.

Positive action: Mindfulness is a positive action, in the doing, and in the receipt of its benefits. Cognitive behavioural therapy is a positive action to take control of your thought processes and feelings. In deciding to live a better life, to find and explore your full potential, positivity is the path and the destination. Positive psychology is the understanding and application of positive actions and experiences – to make a good life real.

Positive action is doing the right thing (the positively motivated option over the negative or wrong-footing reaction) – yes – but more than that, positive action is doing something good (something that brings positivity to bear fruit). That is not a judgment on you doing a wrong or bad thing thus far. It is all about getting on the right track, getting the best out of life. It is putting the rewarding (those culminative positive experiences) into your life. Re-righting the boat and sailing into the sunset. Rewriting your narrative to be a happy ending not a horror story. Rewiring the brain to make it so.

One may have heard the axiom 'misery begets misery', well positivity can replicate positivity. The more positivity we generate the more we find it around us. The more tangible it becomes. Positive action is also intent. You might not be feeling positive today but if you smile you can flip that switch. Making a smile instead of a frown connects the positivity circuit, the muscles at the corner of your mouth signal the brain to the expressed emotion. Make a smile now and hold it, become aware of the shape of your smiling mouth, of your cheeks, how it seems to open your eyes and feel that sensation across your face, if you hold it long enough, and it may only take a few seconds you will find you want to smile for real. It's ok to smile for real. The other great thing about smiles is that they are as contagious as yawns, so your smile can make others smile.

We can practise loving kindness with a simple smile. We can energise ourselves with a simple smile. A simple smile is a potent positive action.

The positive actions and exercises in this book are designed to bring you into the now, some of them will take you out of your comfort zone but many will put a smile on your face, if not outright joy in your heart. The positive actions you choose each day will give a sense to the mind-body-spirit of you that you are in happiness mode – that generates well-being and more sensations/awareness of happiness. The more positive experiences, the more positivity experienced.

Positive thinking: Positive thinking is a way to set the default to optimism rather than to pessimism. Some people are a little squeamish about showing optimism, they may infer the connotation of naïveté but the word 'optimism' derives from the Latin word *optimus*, meaning 'best' – and that's all we are doing when we exercise optimism, we are getting the best from the situation. The glass half full not half empty tees one up for awareness and gratitude of what one has and not fear of what one needs/lacks.

Positive thinking can be personal affirmations, can be Neuro Linguistic Programming (NLP), can be all the tips of motivational speakers but it can be simply optimism and that is just choosing (or developing the tendency) to see, acknowledge, believe, expect, intend, or hope that things will turn out well, that all will come right. It is confidence in life and brings with it 'life confidence'.

Positive thinking is not a high wire act without a safety net, rather it is knowing that the safety net is there but also that you have done this a thousand times before, and that all it is, is just walking a straight line, no veering off into rumination and self-doubt – just taking life in your stride. One foot follows the other. This is you, what you do – simple as.

Positive thinking is not about fantasising or day-dreaming idealised futures, it is about seeing the good before you, the positive in the moment or the potential of it in the future. Being cognisant of the positive potential and allowing it manifest and be present. Positive thinking is muscle memory, assurance with the confidence to succeed and to deflect setbacks – it is not absenting oneself from proactive behaviours, or ignoring problems, it is not being so overwhelmed by problems that you can't find solutions or have problem-free periods of life.

Don't worry if you currently think that you are a natural born pessimist – that's just your programming thus far – you can reset yourself. How you make positivity your default setting is to begin by reconsidering or reframing how you define experiences and events. Start by dropping that tendency to dwell on or replay the bad experiences or unpleasant events – instead see that situation as a learning experience. Sometimes the thought may arise that all the effort and hard work has been a waste of time or an epic failure but that's where a positive attitude helps – so if I can quote a fellow Irishman – Samuel Beckett – 'Ever tried. Ever failed. No matter. Try Again. Fail again. Fail better'.

Failing better eventually leads to success. It is how we learn to grip, to crawl, to stand, to talk, to do all human activities from birth. Trial and error, removes the error, hones the skill. Seeing the positive extracting or the good learning opportunity in the misfortune is what brings good fortune – the positive reward. Adopting this mind-set resets the pessimist to an optimist – to the getter of better, to the amasser of positive outcomes.

Optimistic explanatory style: We humans have a natural negative bias, it's a survival instinct, a danger reflex, a cautionary mind-set, that can all too easily exceed its remit and make us hyper-vigilant or over-analytical to all life, not just the snapped twig, the distant growl or the fast-flowing river. We can, through our depressive and anxious experiences, start to search for and overly invest in the potential for bad things to happen. We can shape a narrative of all doom and gloom, all fear and fret and forget that there is better also going on. We don't have to explain the world to ourselves in such negative terms, we can develop a more positive or optimistic outlook.

Exploring more positive narratives, becoming the 'getter of better' is a way to not just see the good going on but to begin to perceive any encountered negative events as temporary and eventually as atypical. Sticking with a pessimistic explanatory style is keeping us in the frame of negative events at high frequency – as typical – even as poor me.

Much of 'the reframing' contained within this book is about learning a new story, one where we are not the victim. Changing our self-perception is a way to alter our interaction with the world, a way to reset our life on a positive track. 'Typical, it's another dreary day' is a pessimistic style. 'Sunshine follows gloom' that's an optimistic style.

Flow: Mihaly Csikszentmihalyi coined the term 'flow' to describe a positive psychological state where one is removed from one's woes, worries and distractions via participation or immersion within a rewarding activity – a sort of peak experience or in the moment experience. It is the 'lost in the garden', 'the skin in the game', the joy of the hobby or the doing of the deed with full focus and purity of intent. It is the expression of your passion or the mastery of your skill – being in the flow of it or at one with it.

It is not zoned out, it is tuned in; there is intense and focused concentration on the task at hand and the present moment, you are fully present in your actions and the moment to moment of the participation – reflective self-consciousness takes a backseat. It is rewarding and releasing. Being in the flow is an experience and expression of your unhindered self, it is dynamic and contributing to a sense of personal well-being and accomplishment. It may be found in meditation, in doing a jigsaw, in walking in the woods, in all aspects of a lived life that's lived well.

Savouring: Positive psychologists Fred Bryant and Joseph Veroff define savouring as 'noticing and appreciating the positive aspects of life'. It is not just getting the goodness out of it, it is getting into it, relishing the moment, thoroughly enjoying it. Savouring is reaping the rewards to the maximum. It is much more than an enjoyment of a pleasure or positive moment; it is finding the aaahhhhh and awe in that moment.

Savouring is often presented as a positive counterpart to coping but it is more than a coping strategy or supportive tool, it is the up-regulation of positive feelings/experiences. It is a retraining, a reframing, a regeneration of the spirit, a relishing of the positive moment – of the goodness abounding, a true sustained appreciation of the good going on. It is more than gratitude, it is more than enjoyment, it is more than just bearing witness, it is meeting the moment of your own flourishing self and letting it be expressed and felt.

Positive virtues and character strengths: In Positive psychology there are six classes of virtues, borrowed from the tenants of major religions and the oldest of philosophical traditions, which collectively are made up of twenty-four core character strengths – adding up to a universal human value system and to a personal etiquette as well as a tool kit for a more sustained authentic and meaningful life. Throughout this book, you will be prompted to explore those virtues and strengths. These virtues are not value judgements, they are tools:

The virtue of Wisdom (knowledge) encompasses the strengths of creativity/expression, curiosity, open-mindedness, love of learning, perspective.

The virtue of Courage encompasses the strengths of bravery, persistence, integrity, vitality/zest for life.

The virtue of Humanity encompasses the strengths of love, kindness, social intelligence.

The virtue of Justice encompasses the strengths of fairness, leadership and active citizenship/social responsibility.

The virtue of Temperance encompasses the strengths of prudence/judiciousness, self-regulation/self-control, forgiveness and mercy, humility and modesty.

The virtue of Transcendence encompasses the strengths of gratitude, hope, appreciation of beauty/respect for excellence, humour/joyousness, spirituality (sense of purpose/connection).

Neuroplasticity: Mindfulness, Cognitive Behavioural Therapies and Positive psychology, all rely on the capacity of your brain to experience and learn from new synaptic firings, new pathways and circuits, to operate new approaches, to incorporate new information and integrate the knowledge and experiences to a more stable and fulfilled life. The brilliant thing is not only is our brain up for the challenge, it is built for it.

Our cerebral neurons and neural networks regularly reorganise their connections and behaviour (impulses, signalling, reactions, computations) in response to new information, on-going learning, sensory stimulation, interactions with our environment and in reaction to damage or dysfunction. It is called neuroplasticity – the malleable nature of the brain, the innate capacity to learn and adapt. Every time we interact with our environment or a situation, our brain fires up and wires together related neurons, it makes the connections in relation to the experience, in response to the stimuli; it is how we record experience and learn to behave/respond to that experience/situation. It is learning to walk, to talk, fire is hot, rain is wet, learning to become and be.

It provides the capacity to not only adapt and survive, but to adapt and thrive. It is our own capability to change. We are not stuck in a mind-set for ever, cursed with a brain that only perceives doom and gloom, pain and angst, we can rewire our brain to make more positive and life-enriching connections, we can train our thinking self to be on the side of our self. The 'plasticity' is the key; our brains are malleable, so if we have thus far trained it to a negative bias, we can retrain it to a different setting. We can train it to let go or overcome past traumatic events, to navigate the on-going vicissitudes of life, to drop negative thought processes and avoidance behaviours which hold us back from living your life to the fullest, from authentic happiness and genuine peace of mind.

While many of the exercises in this book are aimed at rewiring the brain to a more positive bias, the great news is that doing and learning is a neuroplasticity experience – the more you do and learn, the quicker you can rewire. Learning a new recipe or a poem is strengthening the process, facilitating how you can also learn to respond differently to depressive or anxious triggers. We are made by our experiences. So, if what you do is positive, mindful and healing then that's what your brain becomes, if what you learn is how to be more decisive, measured, grounded and in control then that's how your brain will steer you.

This whole book is about modifying our thought patterns, about rewiring the system and strengthening a more resilient personality. It is not that hard to achieve, we can do it via a positive outlook or a more mindful approach to the simple activities that we do every day – through somethings that we can incorporate (mindful meditations, journalling, prosocial activities) more often. Some we might do for a special occasion, such as going to the funfair or taking an adventure holiday – to excite and broaden our perspective and experience. The new and novel are nurturing and positive experiences for the brain and the spirits.

It is all about living to your full potential, building resilience to negative experiences and enhancing and even creating the more positive experiences. We can be fooled into believing that there is a moral deficiency or lack of drive at our core, and indeed other books by CBT practitioners may refer to faulty thinking or flawed logic, but it is not a judgement on you, it is acknowledging that it doesn't have to be that way. It can change.

It is simply that you may have been learning all the negative reactions, firing up the less helpful, less positive connections – depression and its accompanying anxieties can become the overriding stimulus and hijack your brain and perceptions/interactions of life. This book is about regaining control, and all the techniques in it are ways to relearn joy and fulfilment, to retrain the brain to a well-adapted positive bias; to move beyond pain and suffering and past experience – to become the well-being. Are you up for it?

THE PROVERBS

Teas gréine is gar do dhubhadh

Sunshine follows gloom

Ok, here it is right from the start, the aim and outcome of this book – sunshine returns, the gloom does not last forever. Forgive me if it seems that I am giving the ending away but it's too important to leave it any longer. Sunshine follows gloom – yes sunshine follows gloom. Yes! Yes! Yes!

And after the pain or the gloom passes, there is a new light – there is the ever-replenishing light. No matter how thick the clouds, how dark the overcast, how bruising the rain at the moment, or how heavy the weight of your torment, there is a better moment to come. Yes! Yes! Yes!

This the biggest lesson of all. Your pain and suffering is not permanent. Hold on. The clouds will clear; the sun will come out again. There are cycles in the natural world. There are cycles within the human body. There can be shifts in your emotional experiences too. If your sadness is seasonal, it will dissipate in the next season. If your sadness is situational, situations change. Thoughts and reactions can be modified, brain chemistry can be addressed.

I get that the hardest thing is to wait it out, that impatience, frustration and even anger can arise, but it gets easier with mindfulness and cognitive reframing, you can acquire patience and resilience. Equanimity and control can be yours. This book will provide those skills.

Lao Tzu, the sixth century Chinese philosopher and

forefather of Taoism, once noted that 'If you are depressed you are living in the past. If you are anxious you are living in the future. If you are at peace you are living in the present'. Mindfulness is all about being present (alert to reality) and being in the present or the 'now' – that's living moment to moment in the type of alert reality which brings peace and peace of mind, not rumination or troubling thoughts. Mindfulness is how you can step out of the depression and angst, how you can step into a different moment of being – beyond the troubling.

Entering the now is a timeless zone. You are not aware of how long it is taking for those clouds to shift, for your mood to lift. It is not waiting down the clock, it is living a life as you go. You are in a different awareness with mindfulness. The clouds are still making their way across the sun. You are just not labouring every second in anticipation, or worse – in overshadowed mood. You are experiencing a different moment, a better nowness. The gloom is already getting replaced.

Exercise – entering the now:

Take a deep breath – one of the quickest ways to enter the now is to consciously take a deep breath – you instantly become aware of your physicality. As your lungs fill, your attention is redirected momentarily from your thoughts to the sensation of their expansion. Exhale – let some tension go in the release. Repeat.

This is a distraction away from the panic or distress – a circuit-breaker; it is tricking the brain to shift focus. Often that's enough to dissipate the stressing dynamic. It is like counting to ten … and then resetting yourself to react to the situation differently. It's the switch to taking control.

Take a deeper breath – shifting attention is a great trick; quick and very effective but we can go deeper. I don't mean more lung capacity; I mean more conscious clarity. Breathing patterns are closely connected to emotional states. Both fear and anger can drive fast respiration; to get oxygen to the muscles so you can engage your fight or flight response – we are still primally wired. But on the flip side, relaxation responses also show up in respiration patterns via slow and deepened rhythms and this stabilises blood pressure and heart rate so you can enjoy the downtime moment and recover after the fight or the flight experience. We are primally programmed to recover too.

We will come back to some yogic breathing techniques later in the book but for now take a time out to practise some simple, slow and purposeful inhales and exhales. A few moments of slow and deliberate breathing are a restoration to factory settings. The deep breathing is not just reframing brain perception but body chemistry – lessening adrenalin and cortisol levels, calming the whole system. This is why meditations begin with a focus on breath – it is priming the system for the right response. In finding this calm repose there is no time or headspace to consider clouds above – you are with your true nature – at peace, not perturbed.

An té ná gabhann cómhairle gabhadh sé cómhrac

Whoever will not accept advice must accept strife

This is not a wagging of the finger, it is the sagest of advice – it reminds us that we all need to take advice sometimes – and by take, I mean follow not just hear or read; the word the proverb uses is 'accept' – take that on board. To accept is not just to take it and put it in your pocket for later, it is to integrate it; use it. The other option is to have the strife.

So, it is not just about seeking out advice or receiving advice, it is about the incorporation of advice and positive motivations/strategies into your daily life toward a better lived experience. It is about seeking the knowledge to diminish the power of strife in your life.

The advice of this book is to make certain attitude adjustments and perception shifts to minimise strife, build resilience to strife and ultimately to negate strife. You don't have to eat this sheet of paper in the next ten seconds but the mission is yours to accept.

Exercise – the five acceptances:

Acceptance is not a passivity – it is not accepting your lot willingly, it is recognising your lot and far from relinquishing agency, being one's own sense of self and activations of one's personal motivations, it can be the awakening insight, the call to action, the line in the sand of recognising something exists as a fact, and something needs to be done about it. That may be letting it go and getting on with the rest of your life or it may be making life

55

changes to move beyond strife and push-button triggers. Here are the five acceptances to move forward.

1 – We all need help or support from time to time. There is no denying the truth of this. It may be as simple as an acknowledgement of your circumstance or it may be help to change those circumstances. Accepting that you could do with a little assistance is the door to being helped.

2 – Depression can make us feel quite vulnerable and exposed, and we may have had to build walls around our pain, to shield ourselves from a brutal world or hide our hurting self from others. So it can be hard to drop the defences and accept advice. We need to acknowledge that and accept this is the case, at least some of the time but it doesn't have to be all of the time. By acknowledging, we can move forward.

3 – We may have received a lot of bad advice in the past or had our entreaties for help/support/acknowledgement dismissed and so have hardened against the idea of others as helpful agents. And yes, there are occasions when we have to accept that it wasn't us, it was them. We can acknowledge that without any bitter recriminations, just the reality that not everyone has the right knowledge or interpersonal skills to help. It's just a fact of life.

4 – We can acknowledge and accept that now it's time to find the person or people with the right know-how. To move beyond past hindrances and obstacles and get the knowhow for ourselves. We can accept that we not only need help but will get help. This book might be enough but you have options for expert face to face help via GP referral, professional counsellor, helpline or community support group.

5 – In actively seeking help we are acknowledging the

potential for better is to come. In actively seeking help, we are asserting our agency, acting on our own behalf, we are taking control, we are setting ourselves free, we are manifesting the better. Accept now that better is to come.

Gnáthamh na hoibre an t-eolas

Knowledge comes through practice

This *seanfhocal* is often translated as 'knowledge comes through practice' reminiscent of the old idiom of 'practice makes perfect' and certainly that is a lesson worth paying attention to. The more we do, the better we get at it. We may have spent years becoming proficient and even expert in our depression and self-doubt but we can learn something new, we can get a different outcome via an alternative knowledge – yes, the diligent application of mindfulness, positivity and CBT techniques will reward. We can do more of that, we can perfect those positive practices and not just lighten the load but enlighten the self.

The knowledge of how to defeat our depression will come in the practising of the skills and the mindset adjustments explored and prompted via these proverbs. The ongoing or frequent returning to meditation, journalling, counselling, self-care, etc., all sharpens the sword and strengthens the shield. So we must do it to succeed but it is not just to know the strategy, it is applying it.

The word *gnáthamh* also means routine – we need to make our mental wellbeing and positive experiences as routine, as every day, just as we may have made our psychological woes be so consistent. We can displace the bad with the good. We can become aware of knowing more of the good. We can build a routine of an unstifled life – we can participate in life and thoroughly enjoy it.

Action. The Tao of routine:

So, we could also think of this proverb as a prompt to seek and broaden our self-perception via routine and positive repetitive practices – like zen monks raking a pattern in the gravel, or Christian orders in pursuit of labour that praises God. It is not just that practice makes perfect, but we can set our self to perfect the practice. We can do with the regularity of those things we wish to be consistent in our life – love, laugh, be at peace, experience joy, express gratitude, find stability, be assured, seize the day, be present to our life. We just have got to be in the way of it.

So get a routine – make a plan, it can be a schedule if you wish – but stick to it for a couple of months, make it muscle memory – automatic, the way/how you live. Thereafter you can tweak it to explore more options or to do more of the things that capture your heart or your imagination and drop what might not have worked so well. It could be to have your breakfast orange juice outside every morning – this way you get your dose of vitamin d & c and, even if raining and mid-winter, awaken you immediately to the world beyond your brain. It might be to do five minutes meditation before your shower or every day after lunch. It might be to partake of a yoga class every Wednesday or to try out a new recipe every Saturday.

Routine does not have to be boring; it can be engaging activities – the thing is to stick with the doing – to hone your dedication to the tasks and build your self-discipline. This will yield dividend in all other aspects of your life.

Gáire maith agus codladh fada, an dá leigheas is fearr i leabhar an dochtúra.

A good laugh and a long sleep, the two best cures in the doctor's book.

I have a background in social and therapeutic horticulture, I have written and lectured extensively on the healing potential of gardening and growing our own food and medicines. Whenever I am giving a talk on practical herbalism or more intricate medicinal botany, I will extol the virtues of the natural world and the wealth of phyto-chemicals suited for human health and well-being found there. There is so much of immense benefit growing in our gardens and in the wild and so much that has in the past led to the development of powerful modern medicines and biologics but I will often *caveat* that with the joke that if ever it happens while out on a plant hunting expedition, I was to get bitten by a rabid dog or angered snake, I'll take the helicopter evac and the fifteen belly injections and even the gelatine encased suppository – don't leave me to dig up a purgative root, get me the hell in the air and into a modern medical facility with all the bleeping machines. I can always heal the puncture wounds with some mashed foliage later – but save my life first.

That's not dismissing my belief system or lifetime of learning nor is it abandoning all the science and validation around plant medicines, that is simply acknowledging that in an emergency what is most effective is most efficient. It's ok to skip the rain dance and call the fire brigade to put out the house fire. It's ok to have a plan b. It's ok to take a different route. It's ok to seek the quick fix.

I also say this here, to point out that I am not coming at the approach of this proverb from a very ingrained perspective of holistic over allopathic medicine at all costs. Not at all. I see the value in both. I think we need to work more with whatever from both traditions work best. So, with depression, stress syndromes and our general psychological wellbeing, if there is a pill or herbal tea that will do for you, avail, but there are other options to complement too – many are peppered through this book. There are other factors we can tune into to improve our circumstance. This proverb has two to suggest – laughter and sleep.

Ok 'I'm depressed, I can't laugh'. Not quite true. You might not feel like it but the capacity is there to react to something funny even if it is gallows humour. There were days when I personally wasn't up for interaction let alone gags but a Charlie Brown or Addams family cartoon strip may have yielded a wry smile and that was a positive move to open the door to a chuckle or laugh and a sense of its not as bad as all that.

Of course, you can fake a laugh too – act one out. Your body and brain can't fully tell the difference between the fake laugh and the genuine one, the fake and the real both move muscles that signal the brain to release some happiness chemistry – endorphins. Both will increase intake of oxygen and help to not only stimulate lungs and heart and blood flow but will widen blood vessels, relax muscle tension, lower blood pressure and diminish levels of the stress chemistry – particularly cortisol and epinephrine. A good laugh, real or performed, leaves you feeling more energetic and activated. And on the activated note, it will stimulate the large frontal lobe of our brain responsible for regulation of human emotional responses, strengthening those positive pings.

When it comes to sleep there is a quite complex relationship between quality of sleep and depression. On one hand, lack of sleep can trigger mood changes and prolonged sleep insufficiencies can trigger deeper depression. Depression and anxiety can trigger sleep disturbances. Some may notice a sleep issue before depression, others may observe that the mood changes will slowly alter the sleep patterns, often with daytime fatigue and night-time insomnia. For others it's not so clear cut as to which is the chicken and which the egg but for all of us there is vicious cycle of sleep deprivation or daytime sleepiness contributing to the neurochemical complications that fuel depressive episodes leading to deepening deprivation or, further out of sync sleep patterns.

So, sleep is one of the best medicines for a range of conditions but particularly for depression and anxiety. Disturbances in it should be seen as a comorbidity and addressed as a priority. Maybe that's with resetting of circadian rhythms via daylight exposure, daylight lamps or other light therapy, maybe that's with foods that help balance serotonin or melatonin, maybe it's an herbal treatment such as valerian or chamomile, maybe it is a treatment plan with your GP to restore healthy patterns.

Action. Heads or tails:

This can be a 'heads or tails' coin toss or you can just pick which one you would rather right now. Heads is to get your head down – have a short power nap or a good night's sleep. Tails/tales is go tell a friend a funny story or joke or enjoy some me time with a funny book or comic movie or maybe try out some laughter yoga. The action is to go reap the reward of one of the two best cures. Later you can try the other.

Fearr déanaighe ná ró-dhéanaighe

Better late than never

This proverb derives from a time when Latin was as much a currency of Irish identity as Gaeilge. It derives from the original phrase of Titus Livius, *potiusque sero quam numquam, c.* 27 BC, oft quoted in the hedge schools and soon adopted as a proverbial wisdom. It is a reminder that all is not lost if we soon act. A hint that we can get out of our difficulties or gain reward even if it has been a long time coming. It is an optimistic spin on the long fought, or long delayed, successes. It says 'stick with it'. But first it says do something about it, don't just wait things out, act as quick as you can, even if seemingly late, the doing can make all the difference.

With depression and worrying mindsets, we can often tell ourselves the story that we are too set in our ways or that we have missed the boat – so why try, why keep struggling, why even bother. But it's only a tale to mask our fear or reticence toward change. Sure, life is hard and there are plenty of hurdles and complications and disappointments (even without the ones we make for ourselves), but why continue to stay in the same bad pattern when a few simple changes could revolutionise your life, could give you back a life. Some decisions are better late than never.

If we look closer at the Irish appropriation of this Roman proverb, at what it actually says in its Irish form, we find it says 'it is better late than too late' and that subtle variance makes all the difference – there is an imperative to act, to cease procrastination and not leave it too late to be of use. We can't wait forever for the right moment to appear, wait until you are in a better place to get started, wait until you get beyond this current episode. Start now. Commit now. You are doing it to end your pain – why prolong that outcome?

So don't just do it this week, start today. Start right now. Make the hay while the sun shines, don't wait to cut the silage when the winter rains are flooding the fields. Don't see this proverb as validation of slow action, and think that it hints at it being ok to hang back a little bit more because its ok to be a little late. No, the longer you wait to change the dynamics of your sorrow, the longer you will suffer the sorrow. Take this as a prompt to not leave it any longer. Take it as a directive.

Worry and depression primes us for procrastination, for rumination over action, for feeling over doing, so I get that it can be hard to just hit the motivation drive. But here's how easy it is – you've already hit the button – you have started, you are reading this book and following the actions and exercises. Take this proverb as a further reaffirmation of commitment, to stick with it and reap the rewards. Yes, it is better late than never and definitely preferable to too late, but it is all the better right now – it not only overrides procrastination but to borrow something *a stitch in time saves nine* – expedience improves outcomes.

Exercise – quick procrastination fix:

Quite a lot of the actions and exercises in this book while

being about a very specific thing – stopping rumination, or helping deal with fear, self-harm or perception shifts, also work to tackle procrastination and acquired inaction – all by asking you to do. These exercises encourage motivation, task-setting, problem-solving and achieving resolution outcomes. Slowly but surely, they will undermine hesitancy and self-doubt. But here's a great quick procrastination buster to get the ball rolling.

Think of a beverage. Fix yourself one – you know, go make it. Then drink it. It can be glass of water with a slice of lemon, a chilled lemonade, a cup of tea, pot of coffee, a banana and strawberry milkshake, a super nutrient smoothie. It doesn't matter which. Don't wait. Think, then act. No delay here. Savour the flavour. Enjoy the reward of getting up and doing.

Ok after your beverage. Wash up. Put away. Do it spritely. No messing with you today. You are on it. If you want to take it further – go for it. Pick a chore you've been putting off. Do it. Do it right away. Strengthen your resolve to be super proactive today. Put a laundry load on, make the bed, sweep the floor, tidy the kitchen cupboards, mow the lawn, clear your in box – whatever it is, make it a was – get it done and off the list. In the process of doing, savour the spring clean energy of it. Enjoy the reward of completing it.

Doing is a harvest, delaying is no reward. Doing is doing you good. Action kills stagnation. Action moves those clouds off the sun.

An té nach bhfuil láidir ní folair dó a bheith glic

He who is not strong must be clever

This could be a line from the *Art of War* by Sun Tzu or one from *The Prince* by Niccolò Machiavelli and yes it has that connotation – a machinations strategy – but it's not about conniving, there is no need for duplicity. It is however about winning. It's about winning even when you are weakened. When you are not strong enough for the fight or the daily plight then it is time to really use that brain – to box clever, to not make a slip-up.

You know when you are on top form, not to eat crap, not to answer the phone to disparagers, not to put yourself in the way of harm or allow draining energies into your life but when you are depleted, it is not so easy. The healthy diet can falter, the phone call or email takes on more resonance and before you know it, that referee in your heart is holding up some blurry digits or that retreat bugle call is sounding in your ears. No, it is most important whenever you are in a weak moment or overwhelmed by events that you engage the intellect.

Mindfulness is not just a relaxation technique, it is an energising technique. It is also about dropping a lot of assumptions – the harmful ones, those prejudices that block a true observation of yourself, the world and reality – but it is also about strengthening brain circuitry. Neuroplasticity is about learning the new and so equally about developing beyond the tired old. The positive psychology, mindfulness and CBT in this book are not just breaking the bonds of depression and self-recrimination but building the pathways to a resilient and formidable mindset. Yes, you can bounce back – that's resilience but yes you can also duck, dive, bob and weave, and not get hit at all – that's your formidable self. This is boxing clever.

So, what are your clever options? Have routines, not as oppressive obligations or guilt triggers if occasionally missed but as a framework to your day or week. Structure is important as it can hold the line when you are under attack, so maintaining that daily walk may just yield enough time out, vitamin D and exercise to sustain you through the gruelling rounds. Boxers may cycle, jog or skip their way to stamina, we can easily mindfully walk our way there. By all means, mindfully skip too. Continuing to journal or engaging in analytical exercises can bring clarity to feelings and behaviours and so yield insight to the pattern of punches being thrown, revealing when to duck, what to block and when to deliver your right cross. Live a healthy lifestyle, a mentally healthy one – by enjoying the joyous and the peaceful, there is receipt of the restorative and energising, while simultaneously resisting rumination and avoiding unnecessary misery is conserving your energy for the ring, you know – save it for the real fight.

Exercise. Knowing your strengths:

We often hear 'know your enemy', well, some of us know more about the enemy than we do about ourselves and the point is that it's not just our foe's strengths and weaknesses that can point to the success of the campaign, but grasping our own. Sure, we know our own weaknesses, that's often the daily debrief, that's often the regular collaboration with the enemy, that's the fifth column within. What about our strengths?

A journal entry or a simple kitchen counter list can help clarify the matter. Make a list of your virtues and strong attributes; kind, caring, diligent, generous, etc. I know it can be hard to boast about your skills, especially as most of us with depression and obtrusive thinking are on the introvert end of the scale – which isn't necessarily a weakness. That too can be a strength – that's the resistance, that's the raiding party by stealth, that's your special ops. But today, boast. Take the bushel off your light.

For now, this list is just to take stock of the good qualities you process – we too often forget that there is good in us when the gloom is in play. Remembering those good points can burn off some cloud. Show yourself how good you can shine. Later on, if you are good at being generous, we can use that to break a bond of depression via the benefits of altruism, if you are inquisitive, we can use that too to build more involvement with situations other than depression and demotivation. What you are we will use, you will use, to be more of that positive, to experience the good. These good traits will come in handy. Noting the best in yourself is the start to getting the best out of yourself.

Cuinnibh an cnámh is leanfaidh an madra thú

Keep hold of the bone and the dog will follow you

Rather than being pursued by the dogs of your dark moods why not train them. Why not take control? This proverb is a reminder of the key component of that; to keep your power. This proverb may echo down from a time when the domestication of wild dogs into guard and hunting dogs was a momentous advantage to the survival and development of human society, but its message of controlling situations is no less true today. In fact, to tame our wilder emotions and thoughts we can employ similar tactics.

This is not that we will feed those snarling wolves in the hope they may one day change their response to us. No, we will show who is boss, who controls the food supply, whose side it is best to be on. We can domesticate our wildest fears and our darkest moods – we just have to train them – how ever slowly or painstaking, and in the end will have fine hounds and productive lives together.

Like the best ancestral wisdom there is not just cleverness to it, there is strategy in it; you take control of the bone and you take control of the dog. If we can take control over our triggers and upsets then we can hold power over them, not them over us. The great thing is taking control can be a skill easily learned. We can utilise something as simple as conscious breathing to not just seize control but strengthen the grip.

Exercise – breath control:

At the beginning we looked at how attuning to your breathing can be both grounding and a circuit-breaker on stress and distress. Ancient wisdom and modern neuroscience reveal that a more 'conscious' or 'mindful' approach to breathing, deepens serenity and positive experience. It is not that you need to exert in your respiration, it is simply that you observe it and by bringing your alert presence to following your breath – inhale, exhale, inhale, exhale – you not only bring your attention into the natural peace of your inner being but build a framework of neural pathways that help to better control your responses to your outer world too.

Breath is not just life; it is control over the vicissitudes of life. Sure, we can take a deep breathe to halt the thought signalling but by breathing as a meditation we can take ourselves out of the situation or triggering moment into a more controlled moment. By taking notice of the breathing as a moment-to-moment experience, we enter the now, not the fray. The more we enter the now, the easier we can enter it when we need to. That's the portal to taking or regaining control.

Take a moment now and consciously breathe.

Caora mhór an t-uan i bhfad

A lamb becomes a sheep if you carry it long enough

Some burdens we think are light, some baggage we think we can handle, but in truth we don't need to carry any of it. Even small troubles can acquire a bigger weight when carried for a long time. Lay them down. Lighten your load. Let things go.

This proverb is a call to drop your worry and move on. If you don't drop it, it grows, it gets heavier, and it gets in the way. A lamb weighs just as heavy as a sheep a mile down the road, but worse a lamb becomes a big burdensome sheep 100 miles down the road. The wisdom here is just because you can handle it now doesn't mean you can maintain the weight indefinitely.

Holding on to the past is a conscious decision, you go there. Yes, YOU go there. Dwelling on past events and delving into rumination is the door to reliving it over and over. We may feel that if we let it go, we are undervaluing the significance of the event, but that's just like breaking your arm again every year on the anniversary of the time you fell off your bike. It should make no sense to revisit pain, to carry burdens forward but we go there to make sense of it all or to define ourselves by it – and that's a problem.

Even though it crops up in several psychotherapies, I don't particularly like the term flawed or faulty thinking, to some people it may imply a notion that we are wrong (and so blameworthy) or are perceiving wrongly through ignorance or stubborn intent (and so self-inflicting). We are not perceiving the original wounding event as anything other than a wounding experience but revisiting it repeatedly, that's a mistake we should admit to. The truth is there are no answers there, only more questions, only more re-enactments of the misery. We might think that it is a way to justify or clarify why you are depressed; but what if it keeps you depressed. That is one to rethink. Do you need to replay old traumas, replay without resolution is re-enactment with loaded bullets.

Ok sometimes a memory or moment suddenly comes to you out of the blue, via a cue or trigger event but is it a flash in the pan or do you make a meal of it, i.e. making it seem more important than it really was? Be honest. Seeing it for what it is, is the way to end it. It took me a long time to own up to how much I was investing in my depression and to loosen its grip. I don't say this to invoke or provoke guilt or self-recrimination – that's just more going there. I say this to help get clear of it. Acknowledging that you are carrying a sheep, is the realisation and incentive to put it where it belongs – down on the ground, or indeed, behind you.

Letting go is also a conscious decision, it is not to meekly forget or passively forgive, but you can also forgive and forget if that moves you forward, nor is it to condone what happened or take the blame for it, it is to stop *collaborating* with that painful experience. Why regularly relive it? Why be stuck in the past? Why be immobilised by painful feelings or held hostage to hurtful memories? Why carry all that pain? Why self-harm?

Letting it go is not going there. Letting it go is letting yourself move on from the painful feelings. Letting go is freeing yourself from the injuries of the past to live a great life now and into the future. And if the closure you need to let go involves a police report, or a *J'Accuse* of any sort then so be it. If it needs a change of address or a new phone number, if it needs a break from social media, or an absence from family events then so be it. Drop the sheep and all its ticks.

Exercise – letting go:

You will need to make the decision to let go. To declutter your life of the hurting past. That's not hiding it in a drawer for later, that's clearing it out altogether. Then you will need to act upon it. Sometimes it is a simple switch that gets flicked in your head, heart or soul – to not hold on to this pain. To make the choice to let it sink back into the past and be over. Other times it is a managed approached of catching the thoughts as they arise, noticing them for what they are – an unhelpful echo – and withdrawing your attention or pinged interest. Mindful exercises, including regular breath meditations, will increase this capacity to notice but not follow up. To come back to your grounded self or go and partake in a different experience.

Here is a simple visualisation to reinforce the power of letting go. Picture yourself in a park or on a large lawn; you are holding a clutch of strings attached to some large, brightly coloured, helium balloons hovering overhead. You have a tight grip but you can feel the pull of the balloons wanting to rise and escape your clutches. Some of your friends and loved ones are there. They look glum. You notice that each balloon has a word printed on it, pain, sorrow, regret, anguish, etc., all the things holding you back. All those things you are holding onto right now.

See the vividness of the balloons, yellow, red, blue, orange, see the emblazoned words, feel the pull of the strings, those balloons really want to obey physics and rise, break free of you and travel on, up, up and away from you. Why not let them? Just open your hand. Watch them rise, up, up and away from you. Higher, higher, out of sight. Gone.

Notice now your friends and love ones, smiling and cheering, releasing their balloons. Happiness abounds. The sky filled with colour. Those balloons rising and disappearing beyond sight. Your world filled with smiling faces. Letting go is not a defeat, it is a celebration.

Ná beannaigh don diabhal go mbeannaí sé duit

Don't greet the devil until he greets you

Brilliant advice from the Christian tradition in Ireland but really it is timeless and universal – don't go looking for trouble. Leave the devil alone, you don't want to be on his radar.

When it comes to depression and our psychological demons, the same advice is worth noting too. Don't go seeking out. In my past, sometimes when I wasn't depressed, I would miss being depressed, I may have been happy to be out of it, but still had a sentimental attachment to being melancholic or worse just felt out of sorts not being in a crisis or a slump – you know, waiting for it to recur and that only cast the spell. 'Speak of the devil' as they say.

Other times the urge and desperation to be free of depression can led us into sensation of seeking risky behaviours. The need to feel. The need to be alive and unbound – at any cost. That's not meeting life head on, that's greeting and old adversary, head long – one well clothed in guilt, shame, remorse and regret. For those of us who struggle with the numbness of depression, the temptation of 'anything but this', or the lure of wanting to catch up on a life having been down, it can turn equally sour. There can be with some of us, a tendency after depression, to try to seize the day, but the grasp may be beyond our reach and we can fall while still off balance and trying to do it all. By all means seek joy, find awe, even *carpe diem* but with the right steadiness, good company or the loving kindness and self-compassion of your better Angels.

Sure this proverb reminds us that we also need to acknowledge the devil whenever he does show up. We can treat him with the respect that any enemy deserves but we don't have to befriend him. A lot of us do feel at home in our darker moods, we have known only that for so long, we may not even notice that we are in the company of a devil. Well we need to treat our depression as we would a toxic parent, a frenemy or a narcissistic relationship and not just consciously reconsider the situation but reverse the hell out of it. Hello – I see you for what you are. Goodbye – I know how you affect me.

We don't need to carry our demons around like a badge of honour or keepsake of our past, if I can hark back to a previous proverb, we can drop them like the lambs that become sheep, like the battering rams they actually are. Then your arms are free to greet life, to carry joy, gratitude and good hope. To not be waving over to devils.

Exercise – how to deal with a devil:

The way to deal with a devil is to recognise him first. There are many types on the depression journey but one that can easily slip in is the draining devil. One of the difficult issues with my own depression was not the beating or hellish torment, it was the periodic bouts of numbness. You can fight the pain, but when feeling nothing it is hard to make a fist and defend yourself, making you feel all the more helpless, all the more detached from life, all the more altered, abnormal or unreal – it is not even 'not feeling', it is feeling out of it altogether. The devil can dispossess as well as possess.

Depressive numbness, aka emotional numbness or that overwhelming sense of being disconnected, has been recoined in recent times – in 2013, the Diagnostic and Statistical Manual of Mental Disorders (DSM-5) classified it as depersonalisation–derealisation disorder (DD). It lists the symptoms as feeling disconnected from one's own body or thoughts (dissociation), feeling detached from the world around you (derealisation), feeling like a stranger, outsider, imposter in one's own life (depersonalisation). All leading to feeling empty, meaningless, worthless, lacking in empathy or concern, in self-care, in autonomy or self-control, sleepwalking through your days, withdrawal from contact and social settings, feeling exhausted or lifeless, experiencing sounds and sights as distorted (dimmer or more grating on the nerves), more questioning or suspicious or untrusting of perceptions and reality, depleted to such a degree as to be opted out or numb to the current circumstance.

The prayers to vanquish that devil are ceremonies of action, or observances of reconnection. They are the rituals of regaining oneself, via engagement with both your inner self and outer world. The recommended coping strategies include reducing stress, regular physical activity, eating a healthy diet, improving sleep hygiene, talking it through with family, friends or a therapist. And yes, they all help alleviate by resetting a focus on doing, on not being stilted or numbed. We can power that up, we can supercharge that, with mindfulness – by bringing as much of our full presence as we can currently muster into the moment, meeting life not greeting devils.

We can power on through with positive psychology,

by savouring that cup of tea, by expressing our creative and thoughtful self in a set of goals for the week, by constructing the day ahead around positive, energising experiences – by not just opting for a coping mechanisms but a behavioural involvement that is the antithesis of depersonalisation or derealisation. Any of the tools at the start of this book, any of the exercises and prompted actions throughout, that's the way to reconnect with your full potential. It can be harder work when feeling depleted, but it is the best ladder out of this particular hell.

Bíonn dhá insint ar scéal agus dhá leagan déag ar amhrán

There are two versions to a story and twelve arrangements to a song

As humans, we are the stories we tell ourselves – there is no getting away from it. It is hard-wired into our brain processes. It is how we learn and how we communicate. Language and storytelling are how we, of all the species of human hominids that evolved on this planet, have survived while others became extinct. But even that is not the full story – we were and are ingenious and creative too – we harnessed technology – not just fire and wheel but the shoe that enabled further travel and the plough-share that allowed us settle when we arrived at more habitable zones.

This proverb reminds us that nothing is so simple and there are complexities at play most of the time. Part of this book is about changing the narrative – especially if the story is doom and gloom, pain and fear. If we can tell ourselves new stories then we can change how we read the room and react to the situations. We can learn to be more confident and competent; we can learn to overcome our past. We can transform ourselves. The song can be rearranged and sweetly sung.

So most of the exercises in this book are about re-writing a positive ending, it is not denying the start, it is not trying to forget the middle, it is about manifesting the next chapter as a powerful next stage in life. It is also in part about looking at the reality of the story. Sometimes all is not what it seems. In finding understanding, we find connection, compassion and healing.

It is often that behind the scenes, the bully is being bullied elsewhere – so the person who may have triggered anxiety or feelings of worthlessness, sorrow or anger in you this week may be going through their own pain. That does not mean that they haven't just been an asshole, you can extend forgiveness and loving kindness if you choose, but you can also just not carry their bad energy into your story. Knowing that it may be all them and not you is liberating. The other version is that you were simply in the wrong time, wrong place and not someone doing wrong or deserving of contempt or a derailing of your day.

The song and the story can have interpretations, you are not denying reality to sing it sweeter, you are not deluding yourself to strive for a happy ending. Sometimes the best thing that you can do is avoid the gloomy songs and the horror stories. Sometimes the best thing you can do is seek the uplifting narratives – the ones that release positive endorphins, that ones that make you feel good.

Exercise – new arrangement:

I am a fan of loving kindness; it is such a beautiful way to turn the tables on depression and agitation. It does not require a lot of physical energy – ok, at the beginning it may require a little psychological heavy lifting, especially if you have long been let down by trust and love or disappointed by friendships and previous support networks. But really there is no reliance on others here, it is just the manifestation of your true self – your own innate essence. Some have called it a generosity of spirit, but you are not giving anything away, you are simply being your full potential.

Loving kindness is an attitude; it is a considered response, a consideration action but it goes beyond adoption of a mindset or approach, it is also a spiritual expression of self. Yes, it is the choice to meet the moment or event with compassion and nonjudgement, but in essence it is meeting with love, it is choosing to experience love in the moment of pain, fear, doubt or agitation. Many practise it as a form of meditation where you not only put aside any negative thoughts/sentiments but allow and experience openness and emotional positivity to arise – to feel the love of the universe, not the hurt of this world – and you extend or dedicate that 'love' to yourself or to others.

Choosing in occasional meditations to extend loving kindness to people in your circle, to strangers in the wider world in distress or even to yourself, will strengthen your capacity to extend loving kindness to unpleasant events in your life. It does mean you learn to love the hurt. You learn to love through the hurt, you learn to love over the hurt. In spite of the hurt. Love becomes the narrative. Make that arrangement with yourself.

I ndiaidh a chéile a thógtar na caisleáin

Castles are built one after the other

In life, no experience is ever wasted, it is all a learning experience, even the bad ones can hold a lesson in how not to repeat them, and the truly terrible ones have a big message in that you have survived it and life goes on beyond it. We humans build upon our experiences, from crawl to walk, from goo-goo-gagga to 'to be or not to be, that is the question'. We have the instinct for it. So, it doesn't have to be heaping pain upon pain, walling ourselves into a prison of anxiety and stress, rumination and shame – it can be building a fortress of resilience and stamina. Pick the good bricks and timbers and build a castle worth occupying.

The lesson of this proverb may stretch back to a time in Irish history when the Anglo-Normans sought to conquer Ireland by very deliberate tactic; take a place, build a castle, defend it. What we Irish learned after we learned how to burn them to the ground was that this 'one castle at a time' mode was much more than an efficiency drive and was indeed a very effective strategy. Thereafter, when we spoke of deliberate steps to success and achievement, we invoked an old harsh lesson – castles are built one after the other.

The sage advice here is to do things one at a time and do each well. No one is saying baby steps. We are building castles – so big leaps can be accomplished but then the trick is to consolidate and hold, don't go rushing on and lose your ground to the locals with a cart of straw, a few logs and some flint. Build the strongest foundation and good structures and hold your ground.

The strong foundations of the castle we want to build lie in meditation; the following one's breath meditation, the mantra or positive affirmation meditations, the visualisation ones, the body scan ones, the sitting, walking, listening ones. Entering the now is the solid reality, the solidest of rock, the start of your kingdom. Meditation is not just a consolidating practice, restoring spirits and energy and clarity of thought, it is a means of transforming the mind – the fortress we seek to own. Meditation not only rewires neural pathways and builds resilience; it encourages positive self-regard and a sense of wellbeing. Quarry those skills. Own that castle.

Exercise – take a seat, own it:

Mindfulness is the opposite to multi-tasking. It is a great way to train the brain to have an alert, focused attention, set on a single task in any given moment. It is a real bastion in protecting your stress levels and defending your mental well-being. Here is a chance to mindfully sit as a meditation – as a strong foundation.

Ok, take a seat. Relax in it. Just sit a moment. Just be a person sitting. Now close your eyes and become more aware of your sitting posture, no need to correct anything. Be at ease. Next, become aware of your feet on the ground, of your bum in the seat, your back against the back rest if there is one. Feel your body rest against that seat, feel that seat hold itself against the shape and weight of your body. You are solid. It is solid. The moment is real, you are truly sitting, the seat is truly being sat upon. Hold that a moment. Experience what it is to sit.

We can often ignore the simple pleasures in life, miss the wonders in the mundane, lose sight of the extra in the ordinary. Sitting is not just for when you are tired, it can be energising, it can be a pure experience in and of itself. By experiencing just sitting, you are not multi-tasking, your brain is not overrun, you can defend your calm from this throne, but you don't even have to adopt a regal pose. Sit however you like – just experience it. Let it be a good moment. The sitter and the seat are one in this moment. Inhale, exhale. Feel the full reality of sitting, let thoughts come and go but observe the sitting self – be in the now of it. A simple action with such a powerful message – you can own the moment and barely lift a finger. Seriously, how powerful is that?

Is minic a ghearr duine slat a bhuail a dhroim féin

A man often cut a stick which beat his own back

Sometimes we are our own downfall. We can go about things the wrong way or we can think about things the absolute wrong way. It's not on purpose; it's a default setting or a learned faulty setting. As you progress through this book all that will begin to change – but just like those previous castles (one at a time) and those knots to be prioritised, we must address the biggest stick – *catastrophising*.

Catastrophising sounds very much like being a drama queen or a tantrum thrower with all the toys flying out of the pram but it is not always an over-the-top reaction, it can just be your current consistent mindset. It is nothing more than mentally going to the worst-case scenario or bleakest picture outcome – but that's nothing short of beating your own back.

Maybe the worst doesn't happen. What then? It reminds me of the old joke about the pessimist and the optimist sitting at the bar and the pessimist says 'Oh my God I don't think this day could get any worse' and the optimist chirps up 'Don't think like that friend, of course it can'. Perspective is often skewed. Making light of it can alter it, making sense of it can correct it. A bad day is a bad day, but it's not necessarily the absolute worst ever.

Ok there are drama queens amongst us – stop over exaggerating – but there are also the fretful or over worrying types – stop magnifying the situation. No point tippy-toeing around it. You are only beating your own back. I don't say this to accuse or to vilify, I say this to let you drop the stick. It took me years to realise I had a stick in my own hand and even then, for a while, I thought the whipping was a necessary part of the process.

Self-reproach may be a switch, regret a rod but the cat-of-nine-tails is catastrophising. Catastrophising is the fast forwarding to the worst possible outcome without really seeing the reality or other possible outcomes, the searching for the reason to beat yourself up today. This is why mindfulness practices are so helpful as they slow the rush to irrationality, they give control and the space to reassess and be less affected – to throw the stick away.

Taking a moment, is taking a moment to realise – to be self-realised in a psychological sense and so respond proportionally rather than enact a kneejerk reaction. The 'call me' text might just mean that the sender has no credit to ring you and they want to share their good news – not 'I'm being followed down a dark lane by a strange scary man with a knife and I am texting this as I frantically look for an escape route, quick ring now or I'll be mugged, murdered or raped, quick, your call will scare him off, hurry, do you want me dead or something, when did you last look at your phone, oh god, you are such a bad person, am I dead already, if only you rang straight back, how will you break it to my family?' Awh the guilt of it all, before you even know it all. The jumped-to assumption, the added layers. That's the catastrophising mind.

The catastrophising mind is also 'I'm never going to recover from this' or the all too common 'I deserve this'. Stop whipping your own back, life is hard enough.

Exercise – stop in the name of love:

In CBT terms, catastrophising is a 'cognitive distortion' and so can be remedied by reframing. There are many ways to carry out some cognitive reframing but a great way to shake up the negative thought perspective is to reveal its flawed logic, that can be hard work sometimes or simply a matter of repeat application. A great trick is to show it up as foolish.

You may have to u-tube or google The Supremes – 'Stop in the name of love' for this one. Having a song or a dance move to pull out of the bag is a good way of putting the negative into the bag. The game here is to tell the thoughts to stop – but with a theme tune or a hand gesture that's amusing and so you fire and wire the laughable (silly) to what should be laughable (dismissed).

So the idea here is to pick one of your recurring worst case scenario thoughts and distort it back – you know the ones, the 'I am such a bad parent, my children will all end up on drugs and hate me' or 'this depression is so terrible it would be better if I killed myself and that would make everyone else happy or relieved to see the back of me'. Both are ridiculous in the cold light of day but depression and angst and past trauma can play terrible tricks with the light. The great thing is, we can trick right back.

So – think that horrible thought out now. Think it again as you sing The Supremes song, or say it out as you make the stop hand gesture. You are not making a fool of yourself, you are showing that 'catastrophe' as nothing more than a clown with a bucket of confetti – there was no water, nobody got wet, tension broken, we all laugh it off.

How often have you screamed 'stop' at these thoughts, inside your head or even out loud? This mockery moment demeans the thought not you, diminishes it, not you. Next time it arises you can shout stop; you can gesture stop, you can sing 'Stop in the name of love'. You can stop its power. The tight, sequined dress is optional.

Leigheas gach brón comhrádh

Conversation is a cure for every sorrow

Poetry, storytelling, and all the oral arts are much appreciated within Irish culture. The use of language to not just paint a picture but conjure a reality, to cast a spell over the moment, is as old as 'the song of Amergin' (considered to be Ireland's first poem from Ireland's first poet) and the art of communication has been a valuable acquisition ever since, from the *seanchaí* to the chat over the fence. It could be noted that while Amergin pronounced, the rest of us conversed. We took the riff and riffed upon it. We made it an interactive experience.

Talk is free flowing in Ireland, it is not small nor cheap, it is cultural currency, it is social bond, it is perhaps even a national identity. So it is no wonder of its magic, there is the potential in it to heal and to heal every sorrow at that. This proverb may remind us that the option of a talking cure is still a real and valid option – that counselling is helpful, not just as a commitment to getting well and staying well but it is a healing process with importance in opening us back up to the world and the support of others. To receive counsel is to take advice but to be in counselling is to communicate your problems and dialogue the steps to resolution. Be it psychoanalysis or CBT or other, those private and sincere conversations can cure our sorrows.

Depression can close us down, remove our capacity to communicate or diminish our perception of being worthy of a voice – so talking is a fight back. It is often that the simple dialogue – the engagement and the exchange, can break the aloneness of your pain, ease the pain of your aloneness and generally loosen the grip of your trouble. The conversation can be a help line chat, a consultation with a GP, a heart to heart with a friend or even just a banal chinwag with a neighbour or colleague. The act of conversing, even about anything but your woes, about nothing at all, can lighten your load, can spark life, hope, positive energy, personal awareness, human connection – all the healing things.

So ... 'What do you think of this weather were having?'

Action. Converse more:

Make three definite approaches this week to hold a conversation – each one that you will fully participate in. It doesn't matter the topic but preferably one other than work or your personal troubles – it is the back and forth that energises the brain, it's the back and forth that lifts the spirits, it's the interaction that soothes the soul. Don't waste the potential of that on hashing up old woes or regurgitating bad news.

This may mean phoning a good friend just to catch up on their goings on. This might be not looking at your phone for the entire taxi ride and instead initiating some banter (light, polite chat) with the driver. It may mean meeting up for a coffee or beer after work with a colleague and not talking shop. It may mean turning up at a community event or even organising one. This is not about getting things off your chest; it is the participation in the prosocial aspect – it is being of a community or communing your humanity.

Conversation is not talking at someone, it is an exchange, interaction – that's listening and hearing and replying, not waiting for them to stop so you can jump in. This is a lost art with many, but let's bring it back. It is such a game changer in the dynamics of your day.

Now if there is something you need to get off your chest do that this week too, with a counsellor or a good friend but please have these non-problem-centred conversations as a priority. Sometimes fixing the problem is about not trying to be all about only fixing the problem. It's good to be outside of that too. There is life beyond your current episode. There is life all around you and always within reach of you. It is often that the life-force is enough to force the sorrow into abatement.

An té nach trua leis do chás, ná déan do ghearán leis

He who does not sympathise with your plight, don't make your complaint to him

At the start of this book, we spoke about the importance of taking advice, well even that must be qualified – it must be good advice. Not everyone who advises has the proper content to deliver or the life experience to qualify their opinions. So many may think that saying 'snap out of it' or 'things could be worse' is just what you need to hear to get yourself motivated or just what they need to say to get the awkward conversation full stopped. They are less than useless. So, who you converse with is key.

This proverb reminds us that we must be selective in whom we share our problems and concerns. We must be judicious in whom we confide and wise about from whom we seek wisdom. Sometimes any shoulder will do, but some shoulders are better to cry on than others. Depression, anxiety, trauma, stress is all too draining to be further drained by an unsympathetic, unhelpful or disparaging person.

There is enough suffering without suffering fools or suffering in front of fools. This does not mean suffer in silence. This means find the right help.

Action. Make a list of good ears:

This doesn't have to be done in ten minutes, you can take the day or even ponder it over the week, but making a list of those who will hear and empathise with your plight is valuable both in knowing whom you can call on and reminding you that there is someone to call up.

Don't include family and friends for the sake of it. Only put down those who you know would improve the situation if you turned up looking for serious help or those who could, without judgement, offer a little tea and sympathy. Leave off the well-intentioned foot-in-mouthers and the clueless but nice. Add to the list helplines and support groups.

It may be for some that the list will only contain helplines and support groups because at present we don't have a circle of people with the right level of emotional intelligence or life experience. That's ok. That's more than ok. That's a list of pure professionals. That's damn good support.

Keep this list safe, having it is knowing you are not so alone in your time of need and if you need to use it, use it. No one on it is a narcissist, no one on it is passive aggressive, no one on there is judgemental, no one on there is a time waster, no one on it is bad listener, everyone on this list will try their best to give you the best advice and support, with genuine purpose and best intentions.

An rud is measa le duine ar domhan n'fheadair sé nach é
lár a leasa é

The very thing a person dreads most in the world could be
the best thing for him

Depression and worrying mindsets don't just steal our joy they can lead us beyond caution and reservation into abject avoidance. Yes abject, as it is not just avoiding the dim lit alley or potential real-life dangers, it is too often, avoiding life altogether. It may be that we are still processing a relationship hurt or we don't want people to find out what we are really like when in a depression or disturbed episode, so we avoid people and social settings, we retreat from the world, and instead of shielding ourselves from further pain we simply deny ourselves opportunities to experience the joys of life – becoming more abject and further detached. That vicious circle needs sorting. You don't have to become the most gregarious person in the world, but a coffee out with a friend, or actually going to the office party this year may just do you the world of good.

Sometimes the biggest dread is owning up to having a problem in the first place. Avoidance is but a short-term strategy, sometimes we need to just go there – confront it and get it out of the way. That may be having the chat with a doctor or opening up to family or friends or just honestly admitting to oneself that there is a problem and that fixing it will free you from it. Once you jump that hurdle, the finishing line is so much closer than you think. Confronting the fear, while unpleasant, is a way to undermine the fear. In cognitive behavioural therapy the saying is 'exposure to fears minimises fears', the premise is that confronting the cause of your fear or dread in stages, a little at a time, eventually interrupts the usual chain reaction of panic and distress around exposure to it. Facing it, faces it down.

This great proverb not only prompts that you try a little exposure but reminds you that the reward is indeed great – the best thing you might ever do.

Exercise – breathe through it, but go/ there ...

This is a sort of flight simulator exercise; we are going to visualise a scenario as a way to put ourselves through it but without any real danger. It's a way of training the brain to cope better with fearful or worrying scenarios.

Go to the place in your house that you feel most safe – the kitchen, the bathroom, the bottom step of the stairs, wherever. Acknowledge this as your safe space. Get comfortable. Using the mindful tool of following your breath (conscious breathing), come to a moment of calm but alert clarity. Now close your eyes and picture your worst fear, be it getting stuck in a lift, in a lift with other people who want to chat, in a lift with germs, or imagine a scenario of that really bad thing you fear most – whatever fuels your anxious rumination.

Just a flash of it, a few fantasy seconds, keep following your breath but notice the dread or the accelerated heart rate. Then open your eyes and keep breathing consciously. Notice you are back home in your safe place. Keep breathing. Acknowledge you are firmly in your safe place and actually safe. No harm has happened. Your brain will register this as a survival of that experience, it will register it too next time – be that in a second visualisation or a real event – as being survivable and so begin to modify your dread perception or panic chain reaction to it. You may still get the adrenalin rush to try to prise open the lift doors, but you won't have the total overwhelming psychological fear as strong as before.

Practise this a few times this week to imprint that you can survive and even become calm in a crisis. By conscious breathing through the simulation, you are wiring with your brain the control of breath and the control of panic/fear. When next in a troubling real-life situation you can use the breath control to achieve a calmed response to the real-life panic/fear.

Léig an donas chun deiridh, a n-dúil s'nach d-tiocaidh se choidche

Leave the bad luck to the last, in hopes that it may never come

This proverb shows the humour that is the resilience of the Irish psyche but don't be too charmed, there is a serious command in it too – leave the bad stuff to the last: *deprioritise* the negative. Too often in life we prioritise or fixate on the negative; that last bad comment or failed exam hangs in the head longer than the several good comments or aced tests or one might spend more head space fantasising about letting that asshole guys' tyres down and forget to conjure a long romantic drive with your loved one. It's as if we are programmed to attend to the bad stuff first – and yes it turns out we are. All humans are.

It is an old caveman survival strategy – the negative bias. We are primed to notice the negative; the cliff edge, the predatory growl in the distance, the change in the weather, the gut feeling, the bad vibe intuition – it kept our ancestors alive. Those with mind-sets and genes that removed the inhibition or caution to run over the cliff or eat the smelly meat or ignore the grimacing raiding party, well they all got edited out of the gene pool. We are the survivors. We carry the attitude, if not the gene, on.

So, on one hand the negative bias is not a really negative thing – only when it goes into overdrive and you starve to death at the back of the cave for fear of sunshine and everything else out here. Anxiety and depression can be negative bias in overdrive, yes there can be reasonable, motivating factors to feeling the way you do but the negative bias thinking keeps it that way longer or trips you into it quicker. We need to tweak that.

Dwelling, rumination, projecting, self-doubt, trepidation, shame, guilt, sadness, unworthiness, whatever it is, what if we simply deprioritise it – left it to last. It might not even arise as we fill the order of the day with positive stuff – as we switch on a positivity bias. This is not ignoring your problems. Don't be the ostrich with the head in the sand and the predator still slowly creeping up on you, be the ostrich taking a leisurely sprint at 70 km/h in their stride – not hanging around for the misfortune but off getting a bit of cardio in. Off prioritising the positive.

Just think, if you were not depressed, anxious or traumatised what would you do. What would you want to do if nothing was holding you back? Start a rock band, travel the world, sweep you know who off their feet? Or just have a quiet life without a worry or regret? Ok – so do that. Book the guitar lessons, pick up the lonely planet guide, put on the feel-good underwear. Or drop your woes. You can't succeed at what you are not doing. Busy yourself with the good stuff and there might just be no room for the bad stuff.

Exercise – prioritise the positive:

This is a simple to do list, a bucket list if you prefer – of all the good things you would like to experience or achieve in life but you are not going to wait until you are close enough to death's door to ring the bell. Start at least one of them today.

Ok, first things first, get at least ten things down on paper, we can modify this list in the future but the first ten things that come to mind, no matter how simple or how improbable. We might even get some of the seemingly improbables done – when I first did this list for myself, my wildest ambition was to get my work published but I had never even sent anything off, I was too busy anticipating rejection to try. So put the big dream down, it may happen, it may be the thing to work toward and the process of putting all the things required in place is the process of accomplishments along the way.

For me, the others to tick included enjoying more nature walks, climb Carrauntoohil, learn to cook, cultivate an edible garden, declutter the bedroom, study Latin. The jury is still out on how well I got on with the culinary arts but *Quot homines, tot sententiae* (There are as many opinions as there are people). It wasn't easy but publishing and all the others eventually happened, not through magical thinking but through application and a switch away from the mindset of self-defeat.

With this list, some may come easily, for others, you will have to make things happen, upskill, take action, to tick off. The list is a to do list. *To do.* It may busy you with incentives, it may give you purpose, reason, ambition. It may catapult you into living a full and varied life. It shows that there is plenty of good to be getting on with. All that dynamics, well that's truly leaving the bad luck to last.

Is leithide an bualtach satail ann

Trampling on dung only spreads it more

Sure, 'shit happens', that's just life but this is one of those cautionary proverbs that reminds us that there is a wrong way to deal with the shit, however it happened. Trampling on it is not the way to go. That may be trampling in rage, which is a waste of energy, and no one comes out of that smelling of roses or it may be that staying in it too long is not a good idea either. We can all step in something from time to time but most will wipe their feet and move on. Some can't but linger. Some can't but go back for a closer look.

This is part of the problem with depression, our programmed negative bias is in constant play and we may be prone to not just feel the shit more when it occurs but actually want to delve into it, perhaps a way to figure out or analyse it but often just because we are familiar with it. We feel we are on home turf; we don't even notice our toes are in the manure.

The problem is that the second we don't wipe our feet and move on, we are already beginning to trample, we are overly investing in our ongoing pain, and it has just become easier to go forensic on the dung hill than go smell the roses a few steps away. And yes, there are people who seem to outright wallow in their misery, it kind of justifies how bad they feel, but imagine putting all that energy into something joyous.

Ok the trampling – the rage or the rumination, is a learned behaviour, it can be put to one side. You don't have to get over invested in every next hurt, you don't have to stay spreading it more.

Action/Exercise. Stepping out of rumination:

Repetitive thinking about the past is known as 'rumination'. Replaying the trauma and tragedies of the past is clinging on to the pain. In fact, it's not only reliving it, it is denying a future life or a real engagement with your present self. Wrongs may have been done, but they don't need to be experienced again and again. They don't have to be trampled in, wallowed in, obsessed over.

Rumination is self-harm. Rumination is the post traumatic wound that can't heal because it is never allowed to scab over. Yes the past may leave a scar but better that than a festering wound. The scar is reminder of recovery. The picked scab or the open wound is just an ongoing dilemma. Enough dilemmas. The past is not the present. You don't have to keep it in the present, you don't have to spread it into your every moment. Step off. Step out of it.

Ok, we may still need to work out some issue or work on some problems but we don't need to always go there. We can be elsewhere. Whenever I am feeling the lure of negative reflection I step into the now – I use a mindful tool to get grounded, to come alive to the wonderful possibilities of life. It is not just that I swap into positive thinking, I jump into positive living. That might be a meditation where I actively opt to radiate joy or reenergise my spiritual/resilient self, that may be cooking a meal, listening to music, going for a bike ride. It is a doing, a be-ing, an engagement with the reality of now. The past is the past, the present is the present. What ever happened in the past is past. What happens in the now, I have control over that.

So today and this week take action. Take control. Mindfully be in the present. Pick a joy and make that joy the moment you experience. Take similar actions anytime you need to break the cycles of rumination, worry and repetitive thinking.

Ní dhéanfaidh smaoineamh an treabhadh duit

You'll never plough a field by turning it over in your mind

We can all overthink things. As depressives and over-thinkers/worriers, we are often more in our head than in the real world. Often that's the very problem; ruminating our way into the next depressive episode, catastrophic thinking our way into deeper angst, turning it over and over in our minds doesn't plough the productive field, no it just bogs us down in the mire.

Sure, there is many a day that we will need to think some things through, but we also need to address and rectify errant thinking – including unhelpful repetitive thinking – and we do that by doing. By engaging with more helpful practices. By putting the work in. By turning the soil, not the thoughts. CBT is not just talking about problems; it is problem-solving. Mindfulness is not emptying the mind of negative thoughts, it is experiencing positive actions. Positive psychology is feeling good while ploughing the field and knowing it is how to cultivate a better existence. We can hitch our plough to those horses.

This proverb is a great call to action – to those good actions. It reminds us that doing is as important as plan-ning. In fact, it's the doing that gets it done. Don't sit there planning to achieve – get up and make achievement happen. Sure, it is good to plan (especially a way out of a problem) and yes, it is important to do the CBT homework or engage the rational intellect to defeat a problem but it is also about action, the movement not the sticking point. Positive action overrides negative thoughts. Repetitive thinking – be it past rumination or future worries – just stops us in our tracks. Action gets the field ploughed.

So don't fear it, don't overthink it, go for it because doing it not only gets it done but gets you past it. Those arduous tasks, that whole field ahead of you, the more you dwell on it, the bigger it gets. Don't procrastinate, don't ruminate, don't lapse into the catastrophising – just make a start to do. A start brings a finish. The field will soon be ploughed.

Action – diminishing catastrophic thinking:

Repetitive thinking about the future is often categorised as 'worry' or 'anxiety projection' but when that worry becomes a downward spiral into ever increasing expectations of worst-case scenarios, it is aptly known as catastrophic thinking. That's living out the dread of a potential shark attack before you even get to the beach, never mind dip in a toe in the water. That's not ploughing the field or sowing the seed because you have been busy rushing forward to the what if there is drought next month, what if the harvest fails in four months, what if the farm goes into foreclosure at the end of the year.

To be 'versed' is to be competent and proficient, it is a term that comes from knowing a poem by heart. Long before the lines of a poem or song became known as a verse, that word meaning 'to turn to the next', related to ploughing of the field. Here are some turns to the next, that we could become well versed in.

Firstly, it is ok to acknowledge that life can be challenging at times and that unpleasant things have and do happen. But in turn we must accept that there are unproblematic days and days where good things happen too.

Secondly, we must notice the pattern of irrational thought. That leap from 'I am not feeling in top form today' to 'I will never ever escape this hell'. We need to turn that too. Just because it's not great at the moment does not mean it is a permanent state. We can in the next pass, focus on a more positive outcome, move into the groove of a less-negative option. We can imprint over the tired old defaults and really plough the field, turn it up to a fine tilth that will take the seeds of positive affirmation, of mindful encounters, of our intent and will to achieve a fruitful harvest to come.

Thirdly, the trick is to keep making the good turn. To get beyond the negativity and on to the next positive section of your life. If you cannot simply let it go and move forward, then it's time to use your thinking brain against unhelpful thoughts; instead of rolling over all the worst that can happen, give a moment of think time to what's the best that could happen. Shift the emphasis. Don't look for where it is all going to go wrong but how you can move beyond or move around. Then move. Keep ploughing on.

Alarm clock malfunction, sour milk on cereal, it's raining out, the car won't start, went for the bike but punctured, ran for the bus but missed it, have to walk, a stone in one shoe, a hole in the other, I am late for work, the rain is turning to sleet – all that doesn't mean it ends in the catastrophe of getting fired for turning up late and wet – maybe it's the funniest story you get to share all week. Maybe the fact that you persevered and got there under such circumstance highlighted your dedication and attracted some well due appreciation. Yes, some days are challenging but don't get stuck in the oh no, strive on for the hell yes – turn the plough, take the rewarding challenge instead.

Ná biodh do theangaidh fa do chrios

Do not keep your tongue under your belt

The urge to not make a scene, leave it be or keep silent is the tyranny of trauma. It may be a defence mechanism, like curling up in ball, you adopt it because you don't want to add attention to your pain, put a spotlight on your shame or throw yourself again in front of blame. Often it is because we were not believed at some point, or were accused of attention seeking or exaggerating or outright lying. We know our truth. But past experience has conditioned a reflex to curl not shout.

I am not saying you have to scream your pain to the world at every opportunity, but don't become totally voiceless, don't suffer in silence, don't take on board the notion of shame or apportion self-blame. Being quiet over time can make some feel like a collaborator with their pre-parators or with the mental illness afflicting – and we may even start berating ourselves with 'I should have spoken up sooner', 'I should have said something', 'Why did I let it happen again?'. Well maybe now is the right time to get your voice back. To speak up or speak out.

Sure it is terrifying but it doesn't have to be a terribly big ordeal – you don't have to take the stand, or paint a placard, or reach for the bullhorn, you can just talk it out; be that with a psychoanalyst, a counsellor, a CBT practitioner, a helpful person on the end of a help line, a good friend. Daring to speak it, breaks its grip of control and suppression. A burden shared is a burden halved. Maybe you do want justice and the placard and stand are legitimate next options but sometimes it is just about having somebody else acknowledge your truth, having somebody else hear it.

It is not just about getting it off your chest, it is getting it out of your soul. It might not be as deep a wound as childhood abuse, addiction or inter-generational trauma, it might just be that you are feeling really down lately about a friendship, relationship or situation and you know if it festers further it will spiral out of control. It is the speaking up that helps all causes. It is the participation with a dialogue that reminds you that you are not alone. The burden halved is an army of one multiplied. The odds just got better. We should have a list of good ears from a previous exercise, is now the time to use it?

Exercise – get a monologue to defeat the inner dialogue:

Sometimes it is your own self putting you in your place. Your inner dialogue repeating 'don't, don't, don't'. We may need to write a new script for that inner critic. It is also the case that if not all your life, then at the least in the days preceding a depressive or anxious episode, you have been listening to the inner voice that reminds you it is time to be depressed or anxious. That inner voice that not only prompts with negative memories but may even list all the ways you deserve this. We are the stories we tell ourselves; they are self-fulfilling prophecies. Sometimes it is hard to stop listening. Well, enough. Change the channel.

In fact, channel something else. To do this effectively I suggest you write and learn a one-minute monologue. Your own power play to replace the drama. Your own good news broadcast to replace the doom, gloom and shame network. It can be in the form of an award acceptance speech; you know one of those where the actor or musician thanks their school teacher for the inspiration. Or it can be a sales pitch – but you are pitching all your positive qualities and past positive experiences as well as future hopes and ambitions. It can be a job interview summary of your skills and don't be shy. It can be a preacher sermon and don't spare the Pentecostal fire.

If it takes a few days to hone it down, that's ok. Have fun with it. Be creative with it. Keep a paper copy or journal it. Read it over a good few times. Practise saying it without reading. Learn it. Learn it by heart. Deliver it to the mirror if you need to. Have it on hand when the inner dialogue needs a flip of the switch.

Yes, it's a circuit-breaker but it is also a positivity re-inforcement. It is not just a channel changer, it's a game changer. It embodies who you are and where you are going. It is the hymn of your positive soul. It is all the stuff worth telling yourself. Converse that to your core. All the angels will applause and even God herself will give you an amen and a hallelujah.

Doras feasa fiafraí

The door to wisdom is asking

The thing is, how do you get an answer if you don't ask the question? And that's not a zen koan (a conundrum used to break from logical thought and provoke enlightenment), that's an immediacy that needs to be comprehended right now, not pondered until a mystical revelation manifests. There is no ambiguity in this proverb – ask. Make it happen! Ok, there is a touch of Matthew 7:7 to it – 'Ask and you shall receive' but there is also the straight forward logic of 'to discover you must explore'. It is not just knocking on the door, its going through it.

Some people may eventually get an epiphany, after years of unchallenged torture and unquestioned stress. A realisation may just occur one day, out of the blue and it all make sense but sometimes a simple 'What the hell is going on? Or 'Why am I here again?' is the door out of your particular hell. Because that first why, generally begs the question of what can be done about it.

Of course, not all questions are to be asked of yourself, but those ones mostly bring forth the answers as to solving the problem of why you are depressed, distressed, repeating unhelpful behaviour, being too raw or too numb to function at a level you wish you could, etc., etc. Some questions are for others; perhaps that's to another who has gone through similar experiences and can give you some good guidance, perhaps it's to your doctor about a meds' review or notes on what else you can do, perhaps that's a 'why?' to a perpetrator from your past or one in your present.

Sometimes the answers will unlock doors, sometimes you won't like the answers that you might hear but even the asking alone is enough to rattle the hinges, to free you from the cage of uncertainty, silence or reticence to move on. There is no onus on a perpetrator to tell you the truth or to not try mess with you further and apportion blame back at you. Sometimes just witnessing that one more lie is enough for you to go live your own truth and cut them out of your narrative. Sometimes the answer is that there is no satisfaction here, no need to waste more time or energy. That's golden wisdom.

Exercise – the Socratic method:

This proverb always reminds me of the Greek philosopher Socrates (470 BC–399 BC) and his attributed quote of 'The unexamined life is not worth living' and of the Socratic method of examining and challenging assumptions in the search for truth and justice which is not a million miles away from challenging assumptions in cognitive behavioural therapy which gets you to a life worth living. The Socratic method, aka Socratic questioning, is a way of challenging philosophical, ethical, legal and even moral assumptions by probing why is it so. 'Why is it so?' is a very effective CBT tool to challenge thoughts and behaviours and help gain insight as well as examine a means of cognitive restructuring through the insight.

The way to question a thought/assumption is to be methodical. It is not a single ask, but a series of questions – a proper investigation. We are seeking to prove it right or wrong by examining its origins and its validity:

1. Is this thought/assumption actually realistic? This is the opening gambit and leads to the next enquiry.
2. Am I basing this thought/opinion on validated facts or upon feelings?
3. What is the evidence for accuracy/trueness of this thought/assumption/feeling?
4. Could I be misinterpreting the evidence, or asserting it without basis?
5. Is this a flawed opinion or invalidated logic?
6. Could I be viewing the situation as black and white, when really its more nuanced or complicated?
7. Is there another way to view the situation?
8. Have I been having these thoughts/assumptions out of habit or by a personal prejudice?
9. Is the thought/assumption still as realistic as when I first questioned it?
10. What use is it to me if it is wrong, inaccurate, harmful or wasting my time with repetitively?

Is doimhin é poll an amhrais

Deep is the hole of doubt

If God is faith, then the Devil is doubt. Doubt undermines belief and not just spiritual belief but, more importantly, self-belief. We often talk about 'our demons' when it comes to substance abuse, sensation seeking, anger issues and other facets of our psychological self that may be less than pleasant. Self-doubt is just as bad, just as limiting, just as detrimental. We need to fill that hole in.

It is hard to get out of a deep hole and it is just as hard to get out of doubt. That said, it gets easier if you stop digging and start reaching up. I know that can sound patronising or preachy, but just as we can paint ourselves into corners, we can dig ourselves into deeper holes. Catastrophic thinking is a sturdy pick and rumination a fine shovel. It is time to lay those burdens down. Can I get an *amen*!

And I mean an *amen* – a 'so be it', a 'let it be done', a 'sin é' on your engagement with doubting thoughts. Enough undermining. It's time to build that ladder or limber up for the climb. The great thing about mindfulness meditation is that it teaches us how to let go of thoughts, how to be free of the need to indulge every whim or maladaptive response. We can stop digging. We can escape the hole.

I am deliberately using religious language in this segment as a way to up the ante, as a way to stir the spirit. It is not a sermon on the mount, it is a sermon to surmount – go surpass, go excel, go get liberated. We can do this through mindfulness, CBT and positive psychology but we can also engage a little faith. Let our spirit sore, feel the power, be the power, have the conviction. Can I get a witness?

So, while I am talking about applying a little faith, it is interesting to note some synonyms of faith – belief, trust, confidence, acceptance – so it doesn't have to be church faith, it can be faith in crystals, faith in meditation, faith in your own innate capacity to strive for better. It doesn't really matter, it's the choosing the higher power over the depths of uncertainty and fear. That's the reaching up. The want to get out from it. That's putting some conviction into going in the direction of 'can' over 'can't'.

There endeth the lesson … or begineth the journey?

Action. Find your spiritual self:

Faith in the religious or spiritual sense is there to give hope, to signpost to better. The parables, teachings and tenants of all faiths have at their core lessons in resilience and mental as well as spiritual self-care and application.

Some of us may no longer trust faith-based systems or religious institutions, and yes it could be argued that world religions seemed to have dug themselves into a hole with a proclivity to predominately moralise rather than edify. Some of us, through years of our pain and suffering, may even have felt abandoned by God. But we don't have to deny ourselves the movement of our spirit, we don't have to abandon our higher power.

I am not part of any religion; I have read up on all and cherry-picked for myself some of the helpful bits (so possibly an official heretic, if not outright heathen) but also I do find as much comfort in a joke shared with a friend as I might once have found in a quiet prayer. I am at one with love and peace in the garden or on a stroll through the woods as at any ceremony or mass. I have lost my given religion but I have found my faith. I know it is prayer to enjoy my joy, to follow my bliss, to exist as my unfettered self. I say this only to highlight there are many paths to heaven, and many ways to be your spiritual self.

So, do this week what brings you joy. Is it singing in the shower, catching a film, musical or play? Making a meal for friends or getting lost in some alone time with a good book. Do it! Do more of what you love, radiate that joy into the world. Occupy yourself with the positive experiences not the self-defeating thoughts. Volunteer at an animal shelter or a food bank, by all means do a litter pick in your local park or fundraise for a local charity – do exercise those higher traits, be that sort of spiritual too.

Whatever it is you do this week; it is to testify to your belief in yourself, in your self's ability to make a difference – to exercise your self-belief and exorcise doubt. Finding your spiritual self doesn't have to be an arduous ask, it is simply you radiating your positive self. That's a life worth living, that's a faith worth keeping.

Is ceirín do gach uile chréacht an fhoighde

Patience is a plaster for all sores

There you have it, patience is the ultimate plaster, time is a healer, achieving distance from the trigger event is the cure. Bid your time well and get well. The proverbial wisdom of the ages, for all ages. Patience will help you overcome.

Patience is not to endure and suffer in silence. Patience is not some polite option. Patience is not an acceptance of or acquiescence to pain and distress. You can get help. You can speak up. You can acquire skills. You can make moves to make things better – all while you wait on the wounds to heal. All while the chrysalis of passing time, distance from the former you, readies you to become anew.

Patience does not negate proactivity. It is in itself a proactive choice. Patience is fortitude. Patience is persistence. Patience is a more resolute self. Whenever I think of patience, I think of the Roman poet Ovid and that great line *Perfer et obdura, dolor hic tibi proderit olim* – Be patient and tough; someday all this pain will be useful to you.

So yes, *Is ceirín do gach uile chréacht an fhoighde* is a stoic sentiment but it is also a tool or mode of behaviour that can diminish the raw wound and prompt a recovered self. In the moment-to-moment meantime, are all the mindful opportunities to awaken perseverance, to awaken to innate resilience and your strong inner self. Patience is applying worry postponement, pain postponement, taking time to journal, attending regular counselling, working methodically though this book or other possible treatment plans. Patience is continuing on. Patience is allowing life to unfold. Patience is not just a virtue; it is health benefit – a plaster for all sores. So yes, bid your time well and get well.

Action. Hone your patience:

The way to acquire patience is to be patient. Beyond your mindfulness, all your conscious listening, conscious tasting, conscious walking and other observed meditations which build both presence and patience, you could explore some pastimes that involve patience. The more exposure to slower pace or having to wait, the more that patient muscle is strengthened – so:

❖ Learn to play the card game known as patience (aka solitaire).
❖ Make a jigsaw.
❖ Knit a scarf.
❖ Watch a tv series or multipart documentary but not by binge-watching, wait a day or a week between episodes.
❖ Learn a new language.
❖ Learn a musical instrument.
❖ Cultivate a vegetable patch.
❖ Make risotto for dinner.
❖ Read up on the stoic philosophers.

Níl leigheas ar an gcathú ach é a mharú le foighne

There is no cure for regret but to kill it with patience

The previous proverb explored patience as a cure for all ills. Here it is for a very specific emotion – regret. Regret plays a big role in the prolonging of a depressive episode as well as often being the initial trigger to an episode. That disappointment or remorse over a recent setback or occurrence can be the thorn prick that allowed infection in, can be the depletion of energy and motivation to get beyond the setback and into the flow of better occurrences. Well, here's how to not just stop it in its tracks, but slay it – have patience.

'Patience' here is the capacity to overcome, the capability to be your resilient self, this minute and into the next, moment-to-moment, ongoing, going forward, not stopped in your tracks. Patience is not the kneejerk reaction; it is the self-control and the fortitude of one's self. Patience is the steadfast power to endure and persist – to acknowledge, continue and thrive beyond each complication met.

In the Irish language *cathú* is a word that can mean temptation, regret or sorrow – the unholy trinity of many a suffering soul. The trick is not to be tempted by prolonged regret, not to indulge it, its ok to experience it, to observe its effect upon your mood and energy levels but it is also ok to let it pass. To not get attached. To remove yourself from it. Don't repent, relent – yield to tolerance, apply forgiveness, allow self-compassion, embrace resilience.

It doesn't have to be a war of attrition, you don't have to wait it out with your life on hold, you can move on with grace, self-compassion and fortitude and live your life with the patient understanding that past regrets don't need a future or a presence in your now.

Impatience is intolerance. Intolerance is exasperation and aggravation. Exasperation and aggravation are irritation, agitation and discontent. Irritation, agitation and discontent are loss of control, annoyance and anxiety – see how it multiplies. Patience is the capacity to not go there, to simply accept and not attach oneself to delay, complication, problems or personal suffering.

We can strengthen our capacity for patience through mediation and other mindful exercises. The more we experience patient and grounded moments the more we attune ourselves to that mode of behaviour.

Exercise – the body scan:

There are a few versions of this, varying in duration, intensity, orientation of progressive focus and also posture (standing, sitting, lying down), but all serve to connect you with your body as a means of mindful engagement, all facilitate a honing of observation skills and learning to focus on real-time experiences. The long-term goal of returning with regularity to this meditation, or scanning process, is to experience with equanimity the body we inhabit and by extension to be able to experience the world and its vicissitudes with equanimity too. It requires some patience but it also strengthens patience.

This version here can begin as a five-minute exercise and stretched out over time to become a ten or fifteen-minute practice. It is a seated version for beginner's ease and it only employs observation, no attempts are made to soothe or solve sensations noticed. Practise it as an observation meditation until you are proficient (not restless within the process), then you can evolve it into a wind down relaxation process or even a progressive muscle relaxation technique. The aim for now is to notice, acknowledge and move on without the need to interfere or alter – to notice, recognise and allow it be of no concern. It is not just acquiring calmed composure, but strengthening of self-control.

So sit comfortably, on a chair or on the floor. There is no pressure to assume any posture other than one you will be able to sustain for five minutes. Take a few breaths and settle into being seated. Close your eyes and follow your breath for a few moments. Bring your attention to the parts of your body that are touching a solid surface, feel your bum on the yoga mat, your back against the wall or supported by the chair rests. Feel your solidity in the posture, be a corporal presence, this is about checking in with your body. Hold that a moment, continue to follow your breathe and as you inhale and exhale be aware that you are of a body, any thoughts that arise let them go, be a body sitting, be yourself sitting.

You may at this point start to feel sensations within the body, a tight neck or a mild lower back ache or feel a pulse in your feet – that's ok, that's just your body saying hello back. We are just going to observe in a systematic way the sections of our body from head to toe or vice versa. There may be no noticeable sensation in some sections – that's ok, there may be pressure, tingling or even temperature noticed in some – that's ok too. The emphasis is on noticing, no need to react. It is a scan through the parts, think of a computer scanner, methodical and unruffled – no judgement or other action, just the process of going through line by line.

Bring your attention to your toes, no need to wiggle just allow your focus/experience to be on your toes, next your feet, your ankles, your calves, resting a few moments on each to check in and be present with, before moving on. Next your thighs, your buttocks, hips, lower back, torso, take as much time as you need with each. Now fingers, wrists, forearms, upper arms, shoulders, observe any sensations present but don't intervene, no need to try relax that area, you are observing the reality of that limb or muscle in the now, it is what it is, you just are, you are there with it, present but unruffled. On to your neck, your jaw, your head, simply scan each, witness, acknowledge, move on, when complete, follow your breathe a few moments, then bring your focus to the entirety of your sitting self, a whole body, your whole self, inhale, exhale, allow yourself to feel solid and grounded, unruffled, just a being sitting, in the moment of sitting and being. Inhale, exhale, there you are, here you are, you *are*, inhale, exhale, slowly open your eyes and when you are ready return to your day.

Ná tabhair thú féin suas don bhrón agus ná bí do do chiapadh féin d'aonghnó

Do not give in to sadness, torment not yourself with brooding

This brilliant proverb is very much a commandment rather than an idiom, but who needs a sweetly put turn of phrase when what you really need is to turn your life around. This is not just the commandment to do it, but how to resist. If you know Irish history, then you know resistance is everything. If you know Irish history and its impact upon the world, then you will know the power of a boycott. Boycott your woes.

Don't give in to sadness reminds us to resist the impulse, learn the techniques to circuit-break feelings or thoughts of sorrow – deflect negativity. *Don't torment yourself with brooding* reminds us that rumination is but a torment, it is only more pain and suffering, it has no good outcome – cease putting yourself in more trouble.

The turning point in my long battle with depression was when I learned to stop playing the film. By that I mean that we can construct a picture of who we are and how we are, based upon our previous experiences and our natural negative bias. We have been depressed and anxious and even traumatised, so we fix that into an image of ourselves and we conform to that portrait by living up to it every day. But it is not just as a snapshot of our story, we can too often let it become the film that we play back repeatedly, deeply ingraining it.

Brooding, rumination and going there daily is how

we project this film into our reality, project it across our today and even into our tomorrow. It literally becomes the only show in town. It gets projected onto every surface, over every experience and scenario, so we only see it – our masterpiece of misery, all our worse bits montaged into 'the worst story ever told!!!' We believe the hype, we fall for the propaganda, we get mesmerised by it.

When I realised that I was queuing up every day to brainwash myself into believing how terrible the world and myself were, it shook me a little, then it shook me up enough to not want another viewing – instead I began to look for a different point of view – a real picture of reality. I stopped giving in to sadness and tormenting myself with brooding – I started living and finding snippets of hope, of lighter moments, of laughter, of calm, of competence, of non-pain, of joy and even awe. And by 'awe' I mean wonder-struck not terror.

It's not that you are trying to force or manufacture a happier film, it's that by dropping the film you get to observe reality and sure some days it rains, some days the sun shines, some days the crooks get away, some days you get the girl or guy in the end, some days you don't. Life won't magically become a rom-com but nor will it be the disaster movie every time.

Action. Get some Awe:

Awe is a spiritual paradigm. Awe is that sense of wonder, that childlike participation with the encountered world that Jesus Christ spoke highly off, that Krishna as a child inhabited, that Buddha knew to appreciate. Awe is meeting everything anew, as if for the first time. It is about being filled with amazement. Awe is awakening from numbness.

We may in the depths of our current suffering not have the energy or enthusiasm to go find some awe but you don't have to do a song and dance to get there – there are gentler, more passive ways to let it simply arise in you. In vocabulary to be 'awestruck' equates with being 'dumbstruck'. How about we commandeer that aspect for fifteen minutes?

Go find a nice place, be it your garden, the local park or the steps of city hall. Somewhere that might be aromatic, visually stimulating, soundful – a babbling brook or a street busy with people makes no difference – go there and sit in silence for fifteen minutes. Look at it, really look at it, take it in, the perfect and the imperfection, the pleasing and the not so pleasing, hear it, smell it, feel it. Life pulsates through it. Life pulsates through you. How amazing is the complexity of life? How is all of this here and what does all of this mean – wow! There now is the awe of it.

Ní bhíonn rath ach mara mbíonn an smacht

There is only success where there is discipline

The champ will tell you that their success is their knockout punch and the will to win, but behind the scenes is the early morning run, the careful diet, the hours upon hours of diligent practice – it's the disciplined life that really won the fight.

This proverb is another Irish gem that reminds us to stick with it, to keep putting into place all those things that equate to a win. That may be journalling, jogging, regular affirmations, daily mindfulness, weekly counselling sessions, whatever stands as a consistent routine of self-care. This is being match fit but it is also the lifestyle of success. You are not just beating your depression or angst; you are living a healthy and fulfilled life.

What I love about this proverb is that it doesn't just remind us that there is discipline behind success, it reminds us that there is 'only success'– there is no room for faltering when discipline or diligence are engaged. This is tough though because discipline is not occasional motivations or intermittent actions, it is continuous application. It is dedication. It involves applying yourself in that direction daily.

When are your worst episodes – when you falter on the regularity of your meds? When you skip sessions? When you go to default approaches to eating, exercise, socialising/communicating? When you forget to float like a butterfly and get stung by the blows of rumination or catastrophic thinking? That is not a guilt trip, that is not an accusation of you being lax, lazy or incapable, it is admission that discipline is hard, that we need to work on it, strengthen its muscles, because we really do need it to keep succeeding.

Action. Consistent success:

Very early in, we looked at the benefit of having a routine to get focused, to manage your depression by having a regular participation with something good, to making positive happenings routine. Perhaps you have been practising one or two since, if you have then great but now is also a good time to expand. If you haven't, now is the time to get that discipline.

Go back to the tools section, pick some disciplines/ practices and try them out this week, add some into your daily routine. Let them work for you. Get the consistent success of the tried and tested. Get the skills and focus to be undefeated.

I am also asking you to develop some hobbies, fitness and prosocial activities than can help bring meaning and purpose to a bad week, and will encourage you to leave the house, or get up, or attend to. Make a list of ones you might like, it can be archery, it could be homebrewing, it could be if you have enjoyed journalling, a creative writer's class. Is cycling hitting the spot or would you like to try judo or rock climbing? Is a book club of interest or are you ready to rumba?

Don't overstretch yourself but make a rota and make it happen. Consistently turn up, you are turning up for you. Do also note the discipline of decent sleep patterns, healthy eating, regular housework – the routines that keep your psychological and physical self in good stead too. To neglect these is to neglect yourself. Discipline, continuance, perseverance, that's sustained success. That's stinging like a bee, not swatted like a fly.

These routines are so much more than busying yourself so that you don't have time for the negative, they are the positive in your life – the repeat positivities that shape the path to 'only success'. They will not only give a rewarding framework to your life; they will let your indomitable spirit shine.

Tá lán mara eile ins an fharraige

There is another tide in the sea

You will have heard of the English proverb 'time and tide waits for no one' – you know, get a move on – seize the day and all that. But apprehension and low mood can stop you in your tracks or slow your best efforts. It is not tardiness on our behalf; it is the genuine physical fatigue and the mental drain that accompanies depression and other stress syndromes. Sure sometimes we can be apathetic (once bitten twice shy) but as often as not, even that is triggered by a depletion of our energies.

Many of us have felt that our depression or angst has held us back in life – blighted all sorts of opportunities, interfered with social life and hampered career advancement. We often beat ourselves up over that – we know deep down we have more potential, that there is more to life but the wind is not in our sails and the tide has gone out too.

What is so important about this proverb is it speaks of second chances. All is not lost. Don't consume yourself with worry or regret, you haven't missed your opportunity completely, be patient, wait, there is a second tide in the sea – there is another chance on the way.

Ok you don't just have to wait, you can get up and walk towards it. You can do what it takes while the tide turns – psychologically speaking you can even make the tide turn.

Action. Go for a walk:

You may have heard the phrase 'walk it off'. That just might be great advice. The story goes that whenever a new client came to the Greek physician Hippocrates (*c.* 460 – *c.* 370 BC), no matter what the complaint was, the prescription was always to go for a walk. If the client came back the next day with the same complaint, the advice was to take a longer walk, if they came back a third time then he would say, 'Ok we have a problem'.

He wasn't the world's most disengaged doctor; he actually viewed walking as a health booster – and he wasn't wrong. The feel-better factor of the walk may be just enough to clear the mind of the current psychosis, or energise the body enough to let the natural endorphins and immune system work their magic, but if the walk didn't do the trick then we had a problem.

I am not saying a walk will instantly cure you of your depressive moments but it can certainly lessen the intensity and frequency of episodes. It can even be a route out of a current predicament. For a start when you are walking you are doing, you are not being upset. Ok you may cry or rage on the walk but ultimately it burns off negative energy and it energises your positive self. When you are walking you are activating your circulation and endorphin release – so the good chemistry gets to the right places.

The walk can be mindful or it can be aerobic. Brisk walks are great, but even a stroll will do. The idea is to get out, get active and not be a hostage to your complaint, let alone to your problem. This sort of proactivity is positive psychology with aerodynamic sneakers on. Use it to figure something out, use it to be distracted by music on your headset or the sights around you as you travel on, you can use it to not think about a thing, you can use it to enter the now.

The walk breaks up the slump of nothingness, eradicates the inertia of demotivation, puts a good action over rawness, numbness or frustration. A walk is reclaiming the will to move on. Of course you can jog on too.

An rud a ghoilleas ar an gcroí caithfidh an t-súil é a shileas

What pains the heart must be washed away with tears

The power of feeling pain and exercising it is important in Irish culture. By exercising I mean physically or demonstrably working it out to rid the energy – or indeed 'exorcise it'. The *caoineadh na marbh* (lament for the dead) carried out at Irish wakes not only expresses grief, it harnesses pain and sorrow and transcends it into performance, it shows it, reveals it, takes it out into the open and in the process pulls from the witnesses of it, their own pain and sorrow.

Between the *caoine* and the *seanfhocal*, there is not a stiff upper lip for grief here. The bottling up of grief and emotion is unhealthy. Equally the wallowing in it is unhealthy – the *caoine* has a time limit (as we will see later). This proverbial gem not only speaks of the acceptable response to pain – through crying or shedding a tear – it also utilises the physical act as a metaphysical tool, to purge the body and psyche of pain. Crying is not an embarrassment, not a failing or a weakness, it is an essential action, sometimes.

Here the pain is washed away by the process of feeling. Whatever about a Tao of grief – 'feeling it' is the 'now' of pain. The moment where your living life meets the full reality of experiencing life; pain or grief is often called bittersweet for this very reason. 'Feeling it' is acknowledgement of the significance of it. Dealing with it right now – not bottling it up – is tackling something in a very mindful way. Meeting the experience full on.

We can have issues with crying, conditioned to think of it as a weakness and often we either defer to numbness to avoid being over-emotional, or we feel guilty, angered or embarrassed about resorting to tears. This proverb reminds us that it is ok to cry, that there is a purpose to it, that it drains from the eye (*sileadh súl*) the pain of the heart. The physical tears are the process of healing – they purge the body of sorrow. It is a process worth engaging with. Crying is a cathartic release.

The other great thing about this proverb is that it reminds us that sorrow is not a life sentence. We can use it up, drain it away, take it off ourselves. You will not feel this way forever. But note 'must' – there is a necessity to act, to do, to process on through. What pains the heart must be dealt with in a very real way. That's not to weep in self-pity, that's not to indulge the misery, it is firmly a conscious acknowledgement of current emotional distress and a first step to getting beyond. Draining the eye is letting go, draining the eye is laying your burdens down, draining the eye is freeing up the soul to soon soar.

I have had bouts of depression from childhood, so long before I found this *seanfhocal*, I knew that depression goes as much as it comes – my experiences taught me that it was cyclical or returning. Soon I would learn that means it is transitory – temporary. Fought or endured, it has a limit – like the cloud shadowing the sun, it is soon enough gone. Yes we can walk to the other hill where the sun is not obscured, we can take control and not mind too much the shadow but we can also let go. Letting go is not always just dropping it, sometimes there needs to be a ritual or process, a few teardrops may be the perfect way to drop the anguish, drop by drop until it is gone. A good cry can do us the world of good. Own it.

And when it's over, look beyond it – the eye has drained the grief, no harm in rewarding it with a trip to a gallery, a sunset, a friendly face. The sister of this proverb is a lovely reminder of a next step – *An rud a líonas an tsúil líoann sé an croí*/What fills the eye fills the heart.

Exercise – Release yourself:

Maybe you can just have a good cry right now and let it all go but not everyone can do that so how about we try a meditation to release the pent-up pain – be that sorrow, angst, anxiety or regret. As we do the release, we can let the emotion go with the freed tension.

Progressive muscle relaxation (PMR) is a physical exercise that triggers a deep relaxation response not just in the muscles worked but psychologically too. It is technique developed by the American Doctor Edmund Jacobson (physician and psychiatrist) in the 1920s, utilised to treat certain types of chronic pain and to help control stress and anxiety. It is sometimes referred to as Jacobson's relaxation technique. Jacobson went on to develop biofeedback.

PMR is helpful with depression, insomnia and chronic fatigue syndromes. The technique is similar to the body scan exercise we explored earlier in the book but rather than just tuning into to each muscle group from toe tip to forehead (or vice versa) we progressively tense then release each muscle group as we go. We affect a tension, then unburden it. The focused tightening followed by conscious release triggers a relaxation response. It can be practised sitting or lying down, it is best accomplished in a comfortable location, free of distractions but it can come in handy in the back of a taxi, an elevator, waiting room or anyplace/time you need it.

Simply take a few breaths to gently relax. Allow your whole body to be still. Pick a direction to go in and proceed. I like to work the tension out from my head, down to my toes and imagine as I go that I am clearing the tension and strife out into the floor to be dissipated but that layer is optional, the tighten and loosen motions will do the trick all by themselves.

Breathe as normal. Become aware of your forehead, raise your eyebrows as far as you can go, feel the tension, hold for a few seconds then release, acknowledge that that tension has gone. Move down, clench your eyelids shut, as tight as you can, hold, experience, release, acknowledge. Next open and widen your mouth, as if to exaggerate a yawn or a roar, hold, experience, release and acknowledge. With your neck you can lean your head left until you feel the stretch, hold and release, then do the right lean, hold a moment and release and acknowledge. Raise your shoulder up, toward your ears, as high as you can go, feel the tension, hold for a few seconds then release, acknowledge that that tension has gone.

Pick an arm, stretch it outwards to the side, push it on out, feel its tension, hold a moment then let it become slack again. Next tighten the biceps by making 'the gun-show' move, hold, feel the tension, slacken and feel the release and acknowledge. Now work the hand and fingers by making a tight fist for five seconds and then releasing and acknowledging.

Now the torso. To tighten the chest, take a deep breath and hold, exhale the release, acknowledge the release of tension. For the abdomen simply pull in your stomach, hold a moment and release. Squeeze your buttocks, feel that tension, hold a moment then release and acknowledge.

Pick the left or right leg then squeeze your thigh muscles and after five seconds release, move down to the calf muscle which you can tighten by pulling toes towards you, hold experience, release. Lastly to tense the foot, curl your toes downward, hold and then release and acknowledge. Do the other leg.

End by taking a few relaxing breaths and acknowledging or expressing gratitude for the tension released and the relaxation now triggered.

An rud a líonas an tsúil, líoann sé an croí

What fills the eye, fills the heart

This is a *seanfhocail* that is often equated with the English proverb 'Beauty is in the eye of the beholder' but it is much more than that. It is not about sexual attraction, nor familiarity engendering fondness. It is a reminder that what we see, what we bear witness to, has a strong impact. In the previous proverb we pondered how sorrow can be drained from the eye, here we are asked to consider what emotions we may let in through the eye.

In a positive and mindful sense, it speaks to filling the eye with beauty as a means of opening or filling the heart. It hints at appreciation and gratitude. It is good for us to appreciate beauty – a sunset, an ocean view, the sun through the trees, a dewdrop on a blade of glass, a favourite flower, the faces of our loved ones, those sights and visions that spark serenity, joy, or other positive mood states.

In times of severe stress and deep pain, we often want to retreat from the world and the last thing on our mind is to go buy a bunch of flowers or take a trip to the national gallery. But in looking and admiring we trigger better endorphins that open the possibility to feel a different emotional resonance. And if the picture, or petals, are so beautiful that it prompts a tear to break from our emotional rawness then that's good too – we are not numb in this moment – we are alive to this reality.

We can also take this proverb as a caution too – to be selective in what you let into your heart via your eye. Don't fill yourself with the saddening or distressing when you are already sad or distressed to the brim. So skip the exhibition of the warzone photo-journalists and head straight to the impressionist wing.

In computer science there is a term *GIGO* – *garbage in, garbage out* – a reminder/warning that incorrect, flawed or poor-quality input will only produce incorrect, flawed or poor-quality output – a bad end product. We may hear 'garbage in, garbage out' appropriated by 'healthy eating' gurus and they are right but it is also most appropriate to psychological states.

Everything about being human is the response to stimuli – we wake up to how daylight triggers serotonin release, we get sleepy at the end of the day to how lower light triggers melatonin release. A baby's cry is pitched at the right frequency that you will never sleep through it. We have the negative bias to notice the fast-moving stream or the cliff edge. We have five senses to read the world around us.

If we pollute ourselves with pornography, strong violence films, upsetting scenes on rolling news, then we can start to think that is the world – or worse become desensitised to war, poverty and the ills of society. 'Pollute' sounds moralistic but I genuinely mean that all that negative imagery and depressing messages are a contaminant. Sure bad things are happening, we can't live in a bubble and deny it or worse live in the polluted bubble and only breathe that in – there is good in the world too.

Seeing only the bad, fuels more angst and deeper depression. You wouldn't sit in a room of bad smells all day, so don't pollute your brain with visual garbage. Better still, fill it with delight and positive stimulation.

Action. Get your BIBO on:

This is a challenge to let today be about beauty in, beauty out. Experience the appreciation of a beautiful image or object and take a moment to be grateful for the experience.

Do it mindfully, with alert purpose. Be in the mood of the task, be receptive to the good of it. Now simply take time to admire. Feel how a beautiful object, vista, painting or work of art fills you with a sense of awe. Appreciate that. Let positivity and gratitude fill your heart and fuel the rest of your day.

You could also:

- ❖ Pick some flowers and bring them inside.
- ❖ Make a collage or mood board to illustrate or inspire your mindful intentions or spiritual journey.
- ❖ Enjoy a mindful colouring book.
- ❖ Plant up a window box.
- ❖ Visit a museum, gallery or beauty spot.
- ❖ Change your screen saver to a favourite joyous artwork.

Ar uairibh thigid na hanacraí – is fearr san ná a dteacht an éinfheacht

It is well that misfortunes come – but from time to time and not altogether

We may feel like all this pain and suffering is constant, but even in the bad there is often a moment of good. The trick is to not get so overwhelmed that you can't see or experience the gaps in the supposed onslaught. This may seem the worst week ever, so much so that you forget that you smiled at something funny only this morning, that a good friend rang to check in with you only yesterday, that you are still getting through your day, brushing your teeth, going to school or work, living. That's good – right?

Sure challenging situations and depression can stop you in your tracks and then maybe you can't be bothered to brush your teeth or leave the house, you don't feel you can function but that's just this moment. This moment will pass and you will be in another moment – nothing happens altogether. Life is spaced out. Life goes from moment to moment, from one experience to the next experience. Not every moment will be a misfortune.

Not every crisis has to be a cataclysm. I know it is difficult when you are in it, to see beyond it or even a way around it but how you consider the current crisis is so important to the progression of it, to it becoming just a temporary setback or to it having a lasting impact. Anxious moments don't have to cripple, they can be catalysts for change, depression does not have to blight, it can be a chance to hit the reset button. Misfortunes don't come all at once, you might not be as overwhelmed as it first appears. You may even use the current situation as a springboard to better.

This current crisis can bring an opportunity to turn things in the right direction. I know it's a hard ask to the see the positive in a negative but that's a sure-fire way to undermine the grip of the negative. That's turning the tables on a bad situation, which puts you in a better position. This proverb reminds us that no matter how it may seem, this current issue is a manageable bite. It doesn't have to swallow you up.

Exercise – perception shift:

An opportunity to look for the good in the current bad.

So in this current crisis, what is its silver lining? Are you done enduring it and ready for change? What has all the pain and sorrow taught you? Maybe it's that you are strong enough to endure, maybe it is that you walked yourself into it (no recrimination, just the understanding that you can walk yourself out of it) maybe it is that all these past and recurring experiences have provided you with depth of character.

Bad things happen – but volcanos make new land masses, some plant species regenerate after forest fires, pandemic lockdowns improve air quality. Not all bad is totally bad. This current crisis is redeemable, you can salvage yourself from it. Classic mythology embodies this in the story of the phoenix rising from the flames. We can be such.

Not dwelling on it as the worst thing that will ever

happen or fixating on the inescapable doom of it will give you back a breath, a space to not be so overwhelmed. A space to see it is just the current crisis and make a plan to survive it.

So journal or ponder this quick tick list:

- ❖ Is it temporary – tick.
- ❖ Can I learn something from how I react to it – tick.
- ❖ Can I change how I react to it – tick.
- ❖ Can I minimise the impact – tick.

Ní hé lá na gaoithe lá na scolb

The windy day is not the day for thatching

All through this book I am asking you to get motivated and active against your strife. To solve your problems, tackle the causes of your woe, to be proactive and energetic about achieving and sustaining a more positive and happy life. The intent to do that will reap rewards but I get that some days it may be too turbulent, that we might not have opportunity never mind boundless energy. That's ok, there is even proverbial precedence – *Ní hé lá na gaoithe lá na scolb.*

I love this proverb; it says pick your moment. There will be another opportunity; there will be a more appropriate moment. You are not shirking the work, you are not in avoidance, you are simply acknowledging the reality that it is just too windy to do it right and well. And that's the key – right and well. Keeping your powder dry until it will really count.

So by that token, the day that you are having a cluster of panic attacks is not the day to join the meditation class. The day you are tiggered by intrusive thoughts and self-doubt is not the day to chance the open mic talent night. By all means do the breath work, go for a conscious walk, check the ladder and your other tools but don't get on that roof. Take it as an opportunity to not be under pressure – to power down and just recoup. The day you can't stop crying or feel so fatigued, is not the day to go check out laughter therapy or volunteer at the charity bring and buy – no that day is a self-care day, forget the roof altogether.

I understand that for many, the urge is to keep busy, for fear the thoughts will bubble up, for fear the walls will close in but we need to get used to being with ourselves too. Busy can be an avoidance strategy. Learning to take it easy is also a resilience thing. Sometimes doing nothing is all that can be done. Sometimes doing nothing is everything required – the very thing that needs to be done. The weather will pass, we don't have to be battered by every storm. We can sit some out. We can step out of the way of further damage.

Action. Have a day of rest:

When you have lived a life stifled by depression or angst you can feel guilty about taking a time out, you may feel that you need to catch up on time you've lost to your condition, you may want to prove to others than you are not only in lethargic or halted mode, you want to show your better self not your former weakened state. A time out, a relaxation or a downtime can seem to be more inertia and not the *busy with living* that we may feel we should be, or should be proving to others we are capable of – but really, there is no need to add more complication to your life. This is about dropping that fretting.

We know our depression is not a holiday, it's not an overactive laziness, it's a hell that takes a toll. If others don't get that, that's not our problem. We don't need the negative opinions or misconceptions of others. We don't need to dance to their out of tune rendering. Don't deny yourself a break from your pain. Don't break your neck to prove you are ok.

Today if you can, or on your next available day off –
take a physical rest day, have a duvet day or just a lounge
around in your pyjamas or tracksuit bottoms type of day.
A day where no effort is required. Be grateful for this
opportunity to do nothing today. It is not one enforced
upon you by depression, it is a choice you are making to
be comfortable (and not tormented) in a slowed down
manner.

Spend a little time in your own company. You can
make a jigsaw or bake a cake or catch up on sleep, read
a book you've been waiting to get round to, listen to the
music of your youth, flake out on the couch or lawn chair.
The idea is to lean into minimal exertion and enjoy your
own company. Don't entertain thoughts, just hang out
with yourself.

Use this time too to take a rest from your condition;
take a break from trying to rectify it. Play has been rained
off, health and safety have confiscated the ladder – and
that's ok. So put the feet up, get the head down, binge the
box, look out the window, do the least, conserve energy –
tomorrow may be calm and dry. We can sort the roof then.

Is maith an cúnamh an lá breá

A fine day is a help to everyone

Certainly, a gloomy day can dampen the spirits and a sunny day lift them. It is just the fact that our brains evolved to be active and motivated in daylight and more sedate come evening – these are the circadian rhythms that not only regulate our sleep/wake cycles but control the production and chemical reactions of our neurotransmitters, endorphins and hormones; those molecules that affect the pattern of our moods.

Depression and emotional recrimination can keep us awake at night, keep us indoors during daylight hours and in essence mess with the rhythm and so set off a chain reaction of out of sync increments that alter the pattern of endorphins and neurotransmitter functioning. In the process this just feeds even more into off-kilter responses to wake-sleep cycles and to how we physically as well as mentally feel/experience our day-to-day, our nights, our ever-deepening depression and reactions.

The offset chemistry means we may have more melatonin in the system, actively pinging hunger and comfort eating, if not binge eating and so an extra layer of unhealth and guilt gets added to the equation. The lack or lessening of serotonin is not just a depletion of happy hormones and good mood stability, it also feeds into lower energy and shifts in metabolic health – so actual physical sensations/ manifestations of unwellness. A vicious cycle.

One of the biggest things you do to help undermine your depression, beyond mindset adjustment and self-care, is to reset those circadian rhythms. For some that may be the sole trigger of their low mood and fatigue, for others it is not just a boost, it is a recharging of the energies that will help fuel all those mindset adjustments and self-care actions.

A fine day is a help to everyone but is especially a help to those of us with low mood, with seasonal affected depression and with clinical depression too. The vitamin D is helpful, the serotonin is uplifting but the reset on sleep, metabolic and cellular functioning is restorative.

For some a routine of daylight walks might do it, a daylight bulb or light therapy, taking up gardening or other outside activities, opening the curtains in the morning – the trick is to do it.

Action. Get some good quality daylight:

Pick something off the list and do it or make a similar list and work your way through it over at least one bright day a week for the next few weeks. Make it a thing to take the help that the outside world has to offer:

1. Take a walk around your neighbourhood.
2. Take an excursion to the beach or the hills.
3. Have a picnic over your lunch break.
4. Do some gardening.
5. Try some yoga or tai chi on the lawn or in the park.
6. Go for a cycle.
7. Find a canal, river or lake and skim some stones.
8. Go to the local park and nature watch.
9. Partake in some open-air painting.
10. Sit outside for fifteen minutes and breathe it all in.

Is feárr an mhaith atá ná an dá mhaith a bhí

Better the good thing that is than two good things that were

Now is now. The past is past – both the painful and the comforting. You need to find your mental and emotional wellbeing now – while meditations or psychological exercises to 'find your happy place' are helpful at times, repeatedly dwelling in the past or fantasising the future is a draw away from the now – from living in the present.

Some people believe it really was great in the old days. People were politer, families were closer, neighbourhoods were safer and so on – but was it, or is that just a good excuse to dislike the present, to shy away from the world before you. It is all too easy to opt out of caring or manifesting change now, if it can never be as good as the past. This proverb reminds us to look at the good occurring now and not to drift into nostalgic thinking or get caught up in reminiscing.

Of course, it is good to occasionally reflect on good things from the past, it reminds us that our history was not all pain and trauma but it is even better to acknowledge how well it is going right now. And if it is not going so well right now, if you were distressed or disappointed today or are feeling the physical symptoms of depression, then looking for the good about now can be both a circuit-breaker and a chance to savour the positive vibe, not labour in less productive quarters.

The good thing that is – maybe that you are feeling good today, it may be that it is sunny outside and perfect for a walk or cycle, it may be that it is raining outside and all the local gardens are getting their fill of moisture. Maybe you can hear birdsong, maybe you are going to listen to some of your favourite songs or make a good playlist and make the good moments manifest.

The present can be a very positive place. You could journal the good in your life right now, you could count your blessings on a walk or in a meditation, but you can also just appreciate now – your living self in this moment – there is the positive energy of gratitude and the gift of serenity right here, right now. Grab it.

Action. Make now nicer:

While the proverb is about a perception shift into considering the good of the good, in finding that good thing happening and acknowledging it. Sure, a fine day is a good thing, but there is also genuine good contributing factors in it – reap that too.

That approach prompts that we can also make the now reveal itself as the good that is. We don't have to just alter our mindset and so experience it in more positive manner – that is good but we can be better – we can shape it or at least better frame it for others too. So, make the now nicer for those you encounter today. Be the fine day.

Here are seven ideas to get you started but you can make a longer list. Do them all today in any sequence (tick as you go, if you wish) or make it a week-long action by simply picking one to do on several occasion over the course of today, then tomorrow pick another, and on until all are completed:

1. Be polite today.
2. Connect with family or friends today.
3. Smile to or chat with a neighbour or local shopkeeper.
4. Litter pick or tidy a corner of your street today.
5. Do a random act of kindness for someone at work.
6. Leave a good tip, a thank you note or a nice compliment.
7. Don't say 'have a nice day' say 'isn't it a nice day' – and mean it.

Níl íseal ná uasal ach thíos seal agus thuas seal

There is neither low nor high but down for a while and up for a while

I will return to this theme several times throughout this book, not just because my ancestors sought to codify it so often but because it is perhaps the most important perception shift. It is not just the realisation that you are not stuck in a single perpetual emotion or bound to a pernicious behaviour pattern, not confined to an endless occurrence of depression or low self-esteem, but actually moving through it even as you feel most trapped.

This proverb is most associated with social mobility, the fact that you can move through socio-economic circumstance or at least there was time when a good hunter could become a good king and a small farmer's child become a poet – by merit not lineage or privilege. The caste system in ancient Ireland had flexibility. Today the wise words stand for the fact that situations change.

Life is in flux. Wait a moment and it has changed already. You may believe that you well know that happiness is transient but so too your pain is temporary. This is not a proverb of hope, there is no wait and see, no maybe about it. Instead, it is a proverb of your reality right now – a surety. What you are going through will pass. Knowing that it will change, allows it to begin to change.

When we accept that there is up for a while and down for a while, we can more easily go with the flow of it. That doesn't mean surrender to it, it means take it more in our stride rather the ride white-water rapids of emotional turmoil. We can be at peace that another 'while' is on its way, knowing it will go in that direction means even at our most fatigued and perceived helplessness we are already moving into a better place. We can – with equanimity and not with perturbation.

Equanimity is a state of composure, I often use the term 'to be unruffled'. It is the serenity that comes within mindful practice and from following on with more mindful and aware living. It is the control that comes from CBT and the grounded peace of mind that leads on from positive psychology. It is advanced via many of the exercises in this book.

In the Buddhist tradition there are two aspects of achieving equanimity; *Upekkha* which translates as 'to look over' – this is achieving the insight or perspective to simply observe, recognise it for what it is and to continue unaffected. And *tatramajjhattata* which means 'the middle stance of it all' – this is the decision or mindset of taking up a position of distance (detachment) from the event unfolding – it is the inner calm or self-regulation that allows one to not step forward into the fray or turn to run away; it is simply remaining centred – in the middle but not in the mix. They are two sides of the same coin, they both purchase the same peace, the same awareness that there is neither low not high, just down for a while and up for a while and all the while life goes on.

Exercise – click it (stabilising emotions through self-regulation):

Self-regulation is one of the earliest things we are taught, don't touch the fire, don't snatch the toy from the other child, wait for your soup to cool, or finish your vegetables before the sweet treat. It is the 'wait for it' reflex. It is the patience or the composure to not be frenetic in a commotion or to not make a commotion for no valid reason. It is more than being a good boy or good girl, it is developing self-control and a robust adaptive approach to the vicissitudes of life – a real life skill.

So we have the bones of it already, it may lately have lost some muscle mass, having been back-seated by depression and angst and all their neediness. We might just have to build it back up again. In an adult context it is more about applied attention and redirection. It is taking that same pause between feeling and action we learned as grabby toddlers or scalded lip kids and combining with the opportunity to apply some cognitive reappraisal or reframing of the situation to change our emotional response to it.

You are sensing feelings of sadness, anger, apprehension or are on the cusp of some other emotional moment, but you don't have to let it rise further, you can just hold off on it for this moment, that may be as simple as hitting the pause button and catching your breath and recomposing yourself or it can be changing the channel – swap it out for some focused breathing or positive self-talk.

Self-regulation is applying the perspective of equanimity, not being sucked in. It is taking a moment, leaving some space between situation/thought/feeling and reaction – especially a kneejerk or unfocused response. It is being considerate. It is considering your emotional wellbeing and opting to be well in that moment of your being.

If it helps, utilise an imaginary tv remote control or

simply tap your thumb against the forefinger of the same hand – mime the action and pause or change channel. The playful nature of this can be both a circuit-breaker intervention and mirrors childhood play in a manner that can ignite the powerful early childlike receptivity of the brain – we learn so much in a few short years of infancy and early childhood that tapping into play and child-friendly strategies can power the neural pathways to override the adult reticence to learn new tricks.

Is fearr an té a éiríonn ná an té a thiteas

Better the person who rises up than the one who falls

This proverb may sound at first like a value judgment on those who succeed and those who fail but the context is more in the intention of 'if at first you don't succeed, try again'. A lot of the old proverbs are contractions of longer sayings or contain inferences, this one easily translates as better he who rises than he who is down, but it intimates that the rising part is getting up after a fall or setback. It is a call to be the type of person who gets up to try again and not the one who falls and stays there. It doesn't say it will be easy, it just says it's to be preferred.

'Pick yourself up' is a hard thing to hear especially when you have been demoralised by circumstance and brutalised by experience. But if you don't, who will? Sometimes we can only rely on ourselves – there is a lesson in that too. No shame in it – just more incentive to be resilient and self-reliant. Of course, if there is help – take it. If you are not sure, make your own start – don't wait until after the ten count is over to realise support is not coming.

This proverb is a prompt to keep honing your resilience – that's not your ability to sustain more and more adversity and stress, to take every punch, some days will floor us – but rather it is how to adapt and bounce back from it. Resilience is a combination of a self-discipline, self-assurance and a positive attitude embracing coping strategies and a flexible mindset. It is also a muscle that needs to be trained, becomes the muscle memory response to adversity.

Many of the exercises in this book, from following your breath to progressive muscle relaxation, from journalling to reframing, will develop those skills and build that muscle mass. You will become harder to knock down but if it happens, you will also not be down for as long. The first lesson is that every fall is a chance to stand back up, that every fail is an opportunity to show your resilience and undefeated nature – getting up is the strength – the more you do it, the better at it you get.

Exercise – mastering it:

The American army runs a programme with its recruits known as Master Resilience Training (MRT), to train its soldiers for resilience and adaptive thinking in combat (and outside of it). Much of it stems from a programme first developed to prevent depression and stress syndromes in active service personal. At its core, MRT emphasises the concept/skill of viewing adversity as 'transient, localised, and manageable'. That too is the perception shift this book asks you to take.

MRT competencies include: self-awareness; self-regulation; mental agility; character strengths and optimism. Two sections of the programme are particularly helpful in framing an approach to how we can also master our own resilience: a) avoid thinking traps and b) hunt the good stuff. So for the next week, concertedly deploy those two strategies. Even if you have been doing one or the other already, redouble your energies, hone your focus – achieve the objective.

To 'avoid thinking traps' – recognise and identify

(label) any arising from doubt, rumination, negative inner critiques or other cognitive distortions. Challenge their validity by questioning their basis, are they assumptive, unverified, maladaptive, negative bias, unconstructive, irrational or repetitive – you can even think of them as enemy propaganda. They can be witnessed but not followed, they can be disarmed and left to one side, they can be replaced with more proactive, rational and helpful thinking patterns.

Also set the command to 'hunt the good stuff' – this is not only experiencing some positive experiences but using those positive experiences to challenge or diminish negativity biases. Don't let your negative bias tell you there is no good – even in war, there are the moments you are not under attack, moments of birdsong between bullet fire, the freedom you are fighting for. Hunting the good is looking proactively for the good things that occur each day, it is accumulating the positive as ammunition and curbing the bad. It is also just appreciating the reprieve and maybe this time it is an armistice.

Action. Hunt the good:

If the good is slow to manifest in your life at the minute or if you are stuck in the backend of the darkened cave by context of your mood and behavioural responses, then it might take action to break the rut. It might take a hunt. You just may have to go find the good beyond your immediate vicinity.

Maybe you can visit a scenic area and capture its beauty, get inspired by it, drink it in, take it on board. Maybe while you are there you can paint it, photograph it, write a poem about it. Let its dynamics help make you dynamic again. Maybe you can go be prosocial, be invigorated again by laughter and conversation with friends, family, strangers. Go out for a meal, to the theatre, to a community event, get back around people, join the raiding party to grab some human connections, break the solitude and isolation.

Beyond rut-breaking, hunting the good can become a daily motivation. If 'hunt' seems a little aggressive for you, then 'find the good'. Schedule something each day to experience the lighter side, or the inspiring side, of life. Watch a comedy not a horror. Read a book of poetry not the headlines. Go for a sea swim, a nature walk, a gallery visit. Track down your joy. Follow your bliss. Experience the good of life.

Is maith le Dia féin cúnamh

God himself likes a bit of help

I love this one, to the Irish psyche even the almighty is not above appreciating a helping hand. So good is the power of helping, that God likes to see it happening. So good is it, that God wants you to send some his way. Don't burn me at the stake but amen to that.

So all through this book we have been looking at ways and means of self-help and sometimes that has involved being more prosocial or a degree of community participation. The interactions with others being both a reward and a distraction/circuit-breaker. The helping out, or the participation, is an exercise in not focusing on negativity and breaking free of self-isolating or self-limiting behaviours. This is not just, it is more.

This is the power of being your pure self, which is an interconnected not a disconnected self, one connected/interacting to/with life and the wider world, I would also suggest one interconnected with the spiritual – the 'interbeing' of Buddhism, the 'community of others' as promoted by all faith systems. Just as the microbes at the roots of the tree help that tree derive nutrition from the soil, so falling leaves of that tree replenish the soil that feeds and house those microbes. Call it help, call it support, call it symbiosis, call it inter-being, call it true nature – God is all for it.

One can meditate to be filled with light or imbued with the divine love of God or the healing energy of the universe or however you frame it – of course that's already within us; we can meditate to radiate that outwards and not be diminished by sending it. We can shine a light; we are the light. Even in our darkness, even after our darkness, even in our brightness, we can still offer help, still interconnect.

How about now we put our self firmly into the helping mode – to help others – not just drop our worries but go ease the worries of others. Go do good, go get proactive on higher frequencies and give God a hand.

Action. Help out:

This is not an undertaking for a few days or a week, this is a habit of a lifetime. In retraining our brains away from pain and sorrow we are learning to reach towards joy and gratitude, to find some self-compassion and direct some loving kindness inward and outward. Our depression or past trauma or ongoing circumstances may have made many of us more sympathetic/empathetic and even more considerate and charitable, but it may also have made some of us recoil from the needs of others. In helping, where and when we can, we enrich our spiritual and emotional life. We get to be in the world with others. We get to be a part of a community. This is not about not being so alone; this is about playing your part. This is about being some of that good in the world. This is generating the good that is:

1. Do some volunteer work for a local charity.
2. Raise some funds for a good cause via a sponsored deed (run a marathon or do a marathon read).
3. Start or contribute to a community garden or drop in centre.

4. Support or help organise a tidy team in your locality.
5. Start a share scheme – it could be tools, it might be skills, it could be as simple as books.
6. Carpool or set up a bike loan scheme at work or college.
7. Help out an elderly neighbour – clean the yard, collect a prescription.
8. Make every Wednesday (or day of choice) your personal 'random act of kindness day'.

Gach aon ní mar is cóir, is an pota ar an driosúr!

Everything as it should be, and the pot on the dresser!

This is a proverb that reminds us to be neat and tidy, to have domestic rectitude. It mirrors the English language idiom 'A place for everything, and everything in its place'. We could take it as a call to get psychologically organised – to schedule our mindfulness meditations, CBT exercises and other interventions. To make a plan and stick with it. But we have been doing that anyway – all those actions and exercises – getting the pot on the dresser and the spoons in the drawers.

So instead, let's take it for what it is on the physical plane – a call to tidy up and be well-ordered. Sometimes a physical tidying has a powerful effect on decluttering the mind too: a) you get lost in the action; b) a cleared/decluttered space has associations with competence and being efficient; c) a well arrange room is a breath of fresh air and a much easier space to be mindful or motivated in; d) decluttering is an achievement; the brain recognises that and rewards with positivity endorphins.

When I had my worst times, the dishes and laundry would stack up, the beard would grow out, it was just so hard to get motivated but when I came out of the doldrums and faced a shave and got the place spick and span, I always felt so much better – that's the A–D above. But it is also that we associate with our near environment – so if it's a mess, it is easier for you to be a mess too. Getting everything as it could be is a way to get yourself as you could be.

Exercise – declutter your physical space:

1 **Pinpoint a D-day.** Don't just randomly jump in when you have finished this page – that's only a tidy over. Instead schedule a decluttering day or dedicate an entire weekend to it. This can be a dynamic mindful experience – create the space to savour it, not just labour it. Look at the calendar, circle a day that's good for you to commence and look forward to that day. It might be tomorrow, it might be two weeks away, between now and then get excited about it happening.

2 **Plan of attack.** Is this a solo mission or will you need to rally the troops? If troops, then think now about allotting tasks to skill sets, we are decluttering – that's enough of a whirl, no need for hurt feelings or disarray on the day. If troops, don't forget that they march and declutter on their bellies – stock up on snacks and beverages. Solo or troops, sort your equipment – source boxes and trash bags. Some items will be dumped, others can go to a charity shop. Do you need a colour coded sticker system to pre-identify which is for which pile?

3 **Reconnoitre the enemy positions.** Spend some time looking and considering the objects you own. Decide what is essential to your life or just accumulated stuff. There will be noticeable immediate junk, but also grey areas – that tennis racket under the stairs, will you ever use it, has it strings missing – dump – or is it good to go to a charity shop. Oh, it was grandads and is an heirloom, maybe store it safely and keep for you own grandchildren or just hang it on a wall or shelf to keep out of personal sentimentality, but as ornament or artefact not clutter. Do however limit your sentimentality or that declutter will just be a tidy. You can sticker red to dump, green to charity, blue to figure again on the day.

4 **Access the terrain/plan the outcome.** Maybe you are de-

cluttering a single room or the whole apartment/house. Spend a few minutes to access the decided spaces, look at how they are now and visualise how you would want the area to look post declutter. Picture the perfect room, not just emptied but organised, functional and stylistically suited to your needs and tastes. What doesn't belong in that picture – do a second sweep with the coloured stickers.

5 Secure the perimeter. You will need to set up a base of operations. That's a place to start from. It might be the front porch or the kitchen table – it gets cleared first and from here you can set up your boxes and bags and conduct operations efficiently and effectively.

6 First incursion. Pick a spot, the floor, the walls, the corner shelves, the top of the wardrobe. Clear that location first. Move on.

7 Sustained attack. While every journey begins with a single step, and very war with a single bullet, once the first counter is cleared don't wait for the counter-attack, keep momentum. Not baby steps but defined moves. Don't just rout the junk, clear out all non-essential things. Not everything will go to dump or charity, somethings just need to go back into their right place on the dresser or in the tool box, gym bag, garden shed or book shelf.

8 Smoke 'em if you got 'em. You have subdued if not outright conquered that bedroom, bathroom or garden shed, now take a well-earned break. Take it in the space – grab a pizza, grab a beer, make a cup of tea, sit and survey. Wow you have done good. Catch your breath and savour. If things start to catch your eye, if suddenly you get the spark of genius that that couch would be better at this or that angle and that the tall bookshelf has more candles and kitsch on it than books, then you have to plan for your second attack – unless you are a kitsch collector or a handmade candle-maker. No friendly fire – check your surges of over-enthusiasm.

9 Debrief. At the end of the day – ask yourself 'how did it go?' Is the space as you pictured it would become – as you idealised? Its ok if there is more to be done. You will do it. The path is cleared. The battle won but for a few skirmishes. Meantime, salute the troops, hand out the citations, pin the medals. If solo, slap your own back.

10 **Celebrate victory.** Hard fought and well won. Relish your achievements and fall happily to bed. Sleep easy. The world is a better place. Your cleared room/home is a liberated self.

Ni haon maith a bheith ag caonineadh nuair a imíonn an tsochraid

There's no good in keening when the funeral has moved off

The keen, anglicised from the Gaelic *caoine* – denoting a crying lament, is a function traditionally performed at an Irish wake. Performed is the correct word, for the *caoineadh na marbh* (lament for the dead) is a mourning ritual in the form of a prolonged vocalised cry or wailing of grief, conducted by a group of women skilled in the art and paid to do so. Displaced in recent times to genuine family grief or modern conventions, it was once a normal part of the whole ceremony of death/bereavement.

Its function as a tradition is threefold; the audible lament as a sort of sacred improvised chant marks the loss and sends off the dead – the ritual validates the deceased and initiates their journey on to the otherworld or next portal. The second function of the lament is those performed cries elicit out spontaneous or suppressed cries, the fake tears provoke the real tears of the bereaved and attendees – the cathartic function. Finally, between the performance shared and the outward expression of genuine grief undertaken and collectively experienced, it also has a community-reinforcement role – the sharedness and the commonality of humanity in grief – and importantly marks the deceased as part of a community and guides the community through the loss and continuity, but endurance also, as a bonded group.

Timing is everything and this proverb is about appropriateness of actions and perspective. It speaks of not dragging things beyond their moment. Not to make a meal of it. Not to wallow in the misery. Keening (lamenting) is appropriate at the wake or viewing but when the hearse pulls off and the moment has passed, if you are still keening then who benefits from your display (mock or sincere), not the corpse, not the loved ones, not even yourself.

And when it comes to keening for ourselves, marking our woes, this proverb reminds us that we don't have to be stuck in a loop of perpetual sorrow, we don't have to act out our grief in every moment of our life. There is a saying 'move on'. There is another one 'let go'. The keen or any display of lamentation is fit for purpose when appropriate, the proverb is saying be aware of the context in which you exhibit it – when it will be taken seriously. When it is useful.

We saw earlier that it is good to drain the eye of sorrow, but to be constantly lamenting is an indulgence that hinders recovery. I realise this may sound harsh but lamenting your angst daily will not only tire others of your plight, but drain your own self. Your pain and grief may feel all-consuming but it doesn't have to be, we can through self-regulation and cognitive reframing make it a proportional response, indeed we can even make strides to restrict its control. To let the cortege, move off and we move on.

Exercise – pain postponement:

In the treatment of anxiety there is a technique called worry postponement, it is a practice of apportioning five–

fifteen minutes daily to tackling your fears and worries – it can be via a counselling session or journalling, but the idea is to limit the time investment in your problems. To limit the panic or stress away from hours of your day or even all day, into a manageable bite or a dedicated moment. Later you can wean back even more. Spend less time on it. At first daily, eventually weekly, then only when required. It is a way to not just acquire self-restraint but to deprioritise your suffering and reprioritise living a more varied and less worried life. We can do that with pain too and by that I mean our sorrow.

Many of us need to hold down a job or obligations during strong depression episodes and have managed to mask our hopelessness and regulate our behaviours for those few hours when working. Some of us have had to hide our feelings from family and friends for prolonged periods, even a whole lifetime. So we may have already mastered how to switch it off on command, how to postpone, delay or defer the outward face of our sorrow. The ask now is to *defer* the inner sensations. That's not an ask of blunt will power, that's an acquired skill – a combination of self-regulation and journalling.

Make a decision to journal your feelings every night for the next two weeks, ten minutes or half an hour, that's the time you will go there. This is the planned deferral - actively limiting the impetus to rumination and energy investment until that time. That time is not self-pity time, it is not depths of despair time, it's when you will log how you felt or what occurred, consider if something could have been done differently or just acknowledge that it was a hurtful comment or other trigger that occasioned the feeling or behaviour. It is an opportunity to connect with your emotional self – let it be about self-care not further self-harm.

It is not dismissing or depreciating your feelings, it is regulating the frequency of hurt. This is a framework of allowing yourself to have other parts of the day free from involvement with pain. Emotions that bubble, or behaviours triggered, will still occur during your day but they will become an opportunity to apply self-regulation and mindful tools and then later, at journal time, if they need to be acknowledged, labelled and dealt with, then you have a time limit to safely provide the right attention.

Chun 'uil tuile ó mheud nach d-traoghann

However great the flood, it will ebb

When it comes to despair, we can think it is all-consuming, and yes there are times when it can be a tsunami or a deluge, obliterating all in its path – but floods recede. The proverb is not trying to diminish the damage or dismiss the impact. It is noting that the tide of pain will go out and so beyond the hope of it, there is the reality of it. There will be a chance to recoup and rebuild. There may even be the chance to build more effective flood protection now that you have experienced it.

Sometimes we can think or feel like the only experiences we are having are the negative ones, that we are constantly trying to keep our head above water. We can forget that the tide goes out too. There are sandy beaches as well as choppy waters. It is often difficult while dealing with a strong depressive episode to find a reassuring perspective, to know for certain that it will pass but this proverb reminds us that no matter how great the overwhelming, it will decrease – the greatest of floods ebb.

The trick is to swim in the meantime, not drown. We swim by using the mindful and behavioural tools. They will help us to stay afloat, to get to solid land, to find higher ground, to survive until the crisis abates. We swim by continuing to consciously breathe, continue to observe, stick with the journalling, stroke forward with every positive action and kick hard with all our cognitive reframing.

Exercise – positivity time line:

Take a page and divide it into three sections. Column A is 'past', column B is 'present', column C is 'future'.

To A, add three or four positive things from the past. Passing a test, a first or second kiss, a job promotion, a day you bunked off school and had fun, a concert you enjoyed, a great holiday or adventure – anything that brings a smile, a touch of pride or joy. Big or small, no matter.

To B, add three positives going on right now. Don't falter here, there are some, for starters you have just being smiling about your past. You are actively engaged in your recovery to brighter days, the weather may be good, it may be your day off, or you had a nice lunch and feel good after it. The good is around, if you need to wrack the brain, then wrack. If it just flows then wow, it's a good day.

To C, don't project here, instead intentionally schedule three or four future positive events – it could be one for this evening, something for later in the week, another for some time this month. You don't have to be adventurous, but you don't need to pick the easiest ones either – the criteria is what will bring you joy in an achievable and tangible manner. Catch a comedy show, go out for a meal, book a spa day or go paintballing with friends. It might even be a challenge – learn guitar, take up a hobby or fitness class, get that room decluttered. Picture the positivity surge that will result when these things are accomplished.

This timeline map shows that positivity is an occurrence that you have had and do have and will experience again. It is your past, your present, your future self. Positive happenings have always been a feature of your life. They will be again after the current flood.

Is éascaí nóin ná maidin

Evening is speedier than morning

This proverb correlates with 'Never put off until tomorrow what you can do today'. The 'speedier' bit here is the value of action – it testifies that it is better to do a thing in the evening (this evening) rather than to wait/postpone/prevent until next morning. Why – because life can get in the way. And delaying is not waiting to do, it is not doing.

Having a purpose and accumulating accomplishments in your day is a speedier (and more effective) way to kill off boredom, procrastination, stagnancy, lethargy and apathy. Doing something good is better than feeling something bad. Doing something worthwhile is better than feeling worthless. Filling your evening with actions is in part a distraction from your worries – a time out – but it is not ignoring problems altogether, it is prioritising accomplishment this evening over more regret tomorrow.

It doesn't have to be work, or housework, or a gardening chore, it can be a hobby activity or just getting out and going to a film or for a bike ride. Putting some 'doing' into your being is liberating from emptiness and any potential slide into rumination or other self-harms. So, what action does this evening have in store – what do you need to commence? Have you started that journal, have you still to get your five minutes of mindfulness in, does the laundry need doing?

The way to keep on top of things is to be on it. You don't have to be a harsh taskmaster on yourself, you don't have to run yourself into the ground. You are just not letting things build, tackling what needs to be done as it arises. Staying in control.

Action. Wash some socks:

Washing socks this evening is not only freeing up your to-morrow from sock washing but it is a way to wash those socks with mindfulness; wash only the socks, do them by hand, no thought to other than washing the socks – enjoy or a least be present in the process. Feel the warm water, the texture of the textile, the soft soapiness, the action of washing and ringing out.

It is not a chore. It is a dynamic opportunity. An action meditation. It is living in mindfulness – mindfulness is not all serene meditation, surveying sunsets and having peak experiences, mindfulness is doing the mundane too, experiencing every moment of life as a living being – alive in that moment. Washing the socks is as good an opportunity to get Zen as picking up the gravel rake or gong.

Don't let socks put you off – it's just a jump-off point. You can wash the dog, wash the windows, wash yourself – just be present in it and afterward feel the accomplishment.

Nuair a bhíonn an fíon istigh, bíonn an ciall amuigh

When the wine is in, sense is out.

Once upon a time in Irish history starting from around 1695, laws and reprisals were enacted by the English system in Ireland to halt 'non-conforming' denominations (such as Catholics and Presbyterians) from setting up or attending schools other than English controlled (re-) education centres – the aim was to anglicise the population – not just in the use of the English language but in line with British values and their interpretation of history and politics. A cultural 'ethnic cleansing'.

In reply, the indigenous Irish set up an underground education system known as *scoileanna scairte* – hedge schools – so called as they were often clandestinely convened behind a hedgerow or embankment or secluding ditch. The delivered education was quite classical, continuing to teach through the increasinglu outlawed Irish language, our bardic traditions, folklore and history, alongside geography, reading, writing, mathematics and book-keeping as well as languages – often Latin and Greek through exponents of philosophical thought. So, it is no surprise to find some recycled stoicism crop up in popular *seanfhocail*.

Through study of the classics, the hedge-schooled Irish would have been familiar with *In vino veritas* – in wine lies the truth, a nod to spilling the beans and also *Dove regna il vino non regna il silenzio* – 'Where wine reigns, silence does not reign'. So wine here stands for any alcohol and it is cautionary idiom about the error of too much alcohol consumption and how it can cause problems with your grip on your thoughts and the looseness of your tongue. A danger to all in times of oppression and colonising tactics. Lest we forget the clarion call was 'Ireland sober, Ireland free'. The great lesson in all this is that one can grow from one's oppression and not just suffer under it. Pain and suffering can bring insights too. Insights on strategies to fight back.

I often view depression as a progression enacted with the same ruthless onslaught as the coloniser, systematically stripping all options of self-empowerment and attempting to even crush hope. So in this proverb I also see a caution in the error of self-medication. The drowning of sorrows is no way to swim to safety. I am not saying form a temperance league but be careful when in the midst of a bad situation or episode to not surrender your senses for a temporary relief. And certainly, do not seek out the obliteration of woe via stupor. What quality of life is that?

It is not being prudist or fun-suppressing; it is being responsible to your recovery or well-being. Alcohol and recreational drugs can mess with your brain chemistry, undermine or clash with the chemistry of prescription medication that you may be on for your depression. Alcohol and recreational drugs can put you into complicated situations that you may not be capable of fully discerning or navigating. In other words when you need your senses the most, skip the drop of whatever, it may just drop you further in it.

Exercise – savouring:

Savouring is a way to reconnect with the positivities in your life, to get the maximum joy and reward out of them. Savouring is clasping the mug of coffee with both hands on a chilly morning, inhaling the wakeful aroma, blowing on the surface, anticipating the sip and cherishing each delicious mouthful. Savouring is making something, even as mundane as a morning coffee, into an aaahhhh moment. It is not just experiencing a moment of pleasure; it is paying conscious attention to that pleasurable moment unfolding and drinking in all its goodness. It is fully going there.

Don't just use it on the latte or the long lunch break or the post coital glow, let it flow through and fill other aspects of your life. The idea of savouring positive moments has a strong emphasis in modern Positive Psychology, in a model developed by Fred Bryant and Joseph Veroff they define it as 'the positive counterpart to coping'. So while savouring is an experience of enriched contentment, it can be more, it can be a peak experience. It should be a regular repeat experience, it could be a way to follow your bliss, it is a way to counter-act experiences of pain and sorrow.

Savouring tops up your joy and increases the capacity to experience a sense of well-being. You have savoured in the past, it is a human response, you know how to do it and you know it is not just a cognitive experience but a bodily sensation too; it is all of you, allowing the aaahhhh to resonate. It may be a surrender to the moment, an immersion in the beautiful now of it but it is both you sinking into it and the good sinking into you. It is not only a good experience; it is the experience and incorporation of the good.

Go savour something now; a mug of coffee, a cup of tea, a ripe piece of fruit, a gelato, the aroma or colour of a garden flower, the expanse of the sky, a beautiful piece of music, a favourite film, a cosy sweater, a foot bath, a bubble bath, a bird singing in the distance, the kiss of a loved one, the smile of a friend, a serenity meditation, the satisfaction of having mowed the lawn, even washing the dishes or hanging out the socks to dry. Relish life a little more this week. Savour all the good in it. Be refreshed and replenished by it.

Is fearr rith maith ná droch-sheasamh

A good run is better than a bad stand

This *seanfhocal* is often equated to the English idiom of 'run away and live to fight another day' – other than the flight of the earls, the Irish are not necessarily good at that one. But it is something we should consider, it is not cowardice or dishonour to disengage from the fray, it is often a matter of life and death, it is often the best tactic to withdraw, dress the wounds, gather reserves, generally consolidate and come back to fight tomorrow.

Some days can be overwhelming and time out from the struggle is a good and healthy option, this is not surrender, this is strategy – survival strategy and winning strategy. Too often resilience is spoken of in the context of being a capacity to endure, to take it. But it's actually the capacity to bounce back. It's not about suffering the most, it's about surviving and getting on with your good life. You don't have to brave it out, and let your torso catch every arrow or blow – that's really just a bad stand.

So to a more practical mindful interpretation I see this proverb as a call to physicality; as a dynamic opportunity to fuse physicality and mindfulness. A good run or a brisk walk is better than a bad stand or being a couch potato. Physical exertion is a boost to cognitive function and to personal perception of well-being and emotional health. It can also be done with your full present self – mindfully.

The doing, be it a walk, a jog, a Zumba class, is a time out from woe, the activity helps to take your mind off your troubles and replaces negative experiences with positive ones. The actual activity, the exertion, triggers the release of feel-good endorphins including endogenous cannabinoids which diminish pain, inflammation, stress and tension while boosting mood and perception of well-being. To engage mindfully with your exercise routine or part of it is to fully fuse the good with the moment, to contextualise the positive happening with the reality of your now.

The good run is not away, but toward, a better outcome.

Exercise – run on the spot:

Yeah, I literally mean run on the spot. Seriously, find a quiet corner away from prying eyes or get your family, roommates and even work colleagues, to join in – I dare you. Now, run on the spot. Feel the exertion, feel the elevated heart rate, the new pattern of your breath – this is life, your body is alive. How easy is this to feel yourself present and connected. Thirty seconds will do it. But you can do it any time to energise your attentive mind and your physical body. This is mindfulness in motion not to mention those positive endorphins.

Exercise – circadian cycles:

If you don't own a bike, I suggest you save up and get one. It is not only good for the planet and lessening your carbon emissions but it's a great physical activity that strengthens your physical fitness and mental wellness. All that circulation boost, all those good endorphins, all that increased lung capacity, all that self-empowerment – getting somewhere on your own steam.

Yes, you can cycle mindfully, or to burn off anger or

frustration or troubling thoughts, or to distract or get distance from your woes – cycle as a circuit-breaker or just as way to get some me time. But a daytime cycle, well that's a serotonin boost, that's a way to fit your vitamin D acquisition into a regular routine.

It doesn't have to be daily (brilliant if you can) but you can take the bike out two–three times a week. Be that as the transport option to and from work or as morning or evening exercise. Be that a new weekend hobby to go explore mountain trails or scenic routes.

Is fear leath-builín ná a bheith gan arán

Half a loaf is better than to be without any bread

Do you actually count your blessings, do you measure out your attainment/awareness, do you ever take positive stock? This proverb reminds us to do so. It is not just the optimism of 'a glass half full', that's good in itself, but here in these wise words there is a prompt to not just look on the bright side but to acknowledge actual gratitude for the portion you have of positivity.

Half a loaf makes no difference, it is the portion present right now, there is nothing beyond that portion, you could have even less tomorrow, or much more tomorrow, but neither of those two other outcomes matter, because this portion in front of you is your reality right now. In mindfulness the present is of prime importance, is your principal concern – rather than bemoaning half a loaf, be grateful that you have sustenance now. Eat it mindfully and enjoy its enrichments.

When you are in a depression or frustrated circumstance, it is difficult to switch on a grateful mind-set – you may be thinking what is there to be grateful for, I am in pain, all is torment, there is no way I can muster any positive sentiment around this. But you are not being asked to be grateful for your depression or stress, you are being offered the potential to find respite from your woe by stepping into a positive moment, to be grateful for the covers on your bed, the roof over your head, the breakfast you had – it may be hard to acknowledge but there are positives surrounding you, even in the depths of your despair.

You can even hunt them out; I would force myself to go to a park and appreciate the trees filtering the air, even for just my lungful of sighs, or walk the block, even in a haze, to just get something happening other than confining myself to a room and rumination. I would also be grateful for the duvet that I pulled over my head once I got home. Today I can laugh at the thought of it but those reluctant excursions did diminish the overwhelming and continual experience of depression. No matter how small a gesture, they were some sort of positive sustenance, the half a loaf that fed me.

Being thankful in a depression doesn't disprove that you have been hurt, doesn't lessen the sincerity of your feelings and experiences, it simply validates the good life you also deserve to experience. Amid your angst, any tiny thanks are glimmers of hope, mechanisms of coping, the expression of a different perspective other than total gloom and abject sorrow. Beyond your current angst and on into better times, the regular expression of gratitude or appreciation of the positive unfolding is the building of a psychological immune system, the enhancement of your physical immune system with lowering of blood pressure and stress chemistry. It is the door to optimism, contentment, joy, savouring, self-compassion, generosity and pro-social engagement and even more things to be grateful for.

Exercise – today's blessings today:

I just want you to ponder the good in today, the enrichments of now in the context of now. So, you can contemplate it in your head for a moment or you can make a journal exercise of this and list all that you are grateful for today – it must be specific to today. The context is important.

So for me as I write this, I am often grateful for the roof over my head and the electricity in the sockets that keep the laptop powered and the tea or coffee coming – grateful that I get to work in comfort and enjoy all the processes and routines of it. When I am working outside there are different gratitudes. But specific to now, as I write this in real time, I am grateful for the roof as there is a strong storm brewing outside, my phone is charging in a socket so I can keep contact with family and also emergency services if a tree falls or the river floods, or powerlines go down. I am grateful of my safety and relative comfort. Once upon a time I would have dreaded such a storm, fearing what might happen to loved ones – catastrophising. Now I am on a different wavelength. It's not that I am just not choosing to catastrophise, it is that I have taken positive stock, not only do I not have to climb to higher ground I know I have half a loaf in the cupboard. I know my family are safe and well and I have the means to keep in touch. There is nothing to underpin unnecessary worry. Nothing to trigger despair. My gratitude and acceptance bring control and stability.

Ok your turn. What are the gratitude beatitudes of your now?

Ní troimide an chaora a holann

The sheep does not mind the weight of the wool

The sheep does not notice as a burden, the weight of the wool it carries, the wool is simply a natural extension of its self, it is not a load, it is a protective layer – it is an asset. Some of our best assets are easily carried. Love, compassion, self-respect, hope, gratitude, spiritual awareness – there is no burden in carrying those. So too forgiveness, generosity, humility can be as the wool to the sheep – can be your protective layer.

So there is no burden in carrying a few extra virtues, acquiring some extra cognitive and mindful skills, adding some flexible and clever fibres to our coat – it is only more protective layers, more natural extensions of our true self. Sure, there are burdens we don't need to carry and through this book so far, we have dropped some and will drop more of them but there is no weight at all in the positive acquisition of positive layers.

That's not to say wrap yourself up in cotton wool. We still need to experience the world, all of it, we still need to feel and be human not numbed shells of ourselves. So this is not an invite to make an impenetrable barrier to the realities of life, this is a call to carry also the skillset and mindset to be compassionate, loving, kind, generous, grateful, pleasant, social, interactive and inspiring. Live a full life.

This proverb can also be understood or contemplated in the context of knowledge – many Irish proverbs show the Irish respect and reverence for education. Education is no load, learning is no load, have you learned something new today? Go flex that neuroplasticity.

Action. Read a book:

Ok I know you are reading this one and you may already be a regular reader but ten minutes of reading, that's real reading not scrolling, can reduce stress levels by more than 60%; with the knock on effect of improving mental clarity, immune response and better regulation of inflammation. Depression and inflammation are closely aligned and reading is a real shot in the arm. Any book will do, but something that sparks joy, curiosity or connection will also energise the spirits and soul.

Reading this book and other self-help or motivational books can have a gravity of attention and desire to change attached, so there can be some excitement or emotional investment bouncing about. That's great to get your motivation motivated but to destress I recommend you find a read that is not all about working out your problems but one that's a whole other subject – a real distraction from your woes. A gardening book, a biography of a hero of yours, a guidebook to somewhere you'd love to visit, a book of poetry or a classic of fiction.

So, the ask is, go visit a bookshop or library this week and either pick something at random or something a friend recommended and give it ten minutes of your time there and then. If you liked it, you can borrow or buy, if you didn't like it, no harm, it was only ten minutes and you got your stress reduction in.

Is minic a mhaolaigh béile maith brón

It is often a good meal eased sorrow

This is comfort eating of a different sort. The positive distraction of cooking and eating a meal can break repetitive thought patterns. Sharing of that meal with family and friends can bring levity or even joy to the fore. It mirrors the popular idiom 'all grief is less with bread' (borrowed from Miguel de Cervantes' *Don Quijote de la Mancha*).

It doesn't have to be a pro-social 'breaking of bread' – even a meal for one; a nice lunch or a good dinner can bring a sense of well-being and reward. As the belly fills so too do the energy reserves and even the spiritual reserves. What you eat can even have a further positive effect; there are foods that boost mood or help regulate sleep and tensions.

During a depressive episode, appetite and enjoyment of food can wane, the will or energy to cook can also quickly dissolve and so we do need to take extra care to make sure we are being nourished enough. In some instances, appetite can spike, be that with comfort eating or food cravings – which can be exacerbated by excess melatonin or diminished serotonin caused by daytime naps, avoiding the outside world during daylight and disrupted night-time sleep patterns. Melatonin is not just the sleepy hormone it is a hunger-activating hormone.

Many of us can lean into sweeter and fattier foods, not just in a desperate need for energy but those less healthy food options are generally manufactured to have a 'bliss point' – that's a specific ratio of fat and sugar that gives the brain a little quiver of aaahhhh and so we can end up in a loop of seeking our chemical hit, rather that working to correct, on a more long-term basis, our brain chemistry. Improving your diet can be as helpful as correcting your sleep patterns and thought processes.

Serotonin, dopamine and norepinephrine are neuro-transmitters involved in mental wellness, they are often framed as 'happy hormones' but they are also our 'alert and energetic neurotransmitters'. There are foods that boost their production. Making an appointment with a nutritionist or naturopath can help you incorporate a healthier eating plan into your life. There are also books and cookbooks on the subject. To get you started, fruits, grains, seeds, vegetables as well as prebiotic – and probiotic – rich foods help with serotonin production while protein (including nuts, soy and other vegan sources) triggers dopamine and norepinephrine to be released in the brain. That good meal can ease those sorrows on many levels.

Action. Partake of a good meal:

Cook up a treat or treat yourself to a restaurant visit.

Enjoy the cooking and the eating mindfully. You are nourishing body and soul. Savour it.

If going out to eat then enjoy the whole process; the getting ready, the arriving and being seated, the survey of the menu, the anticipation of your choice, the presentation of expertly cooked fare, the first savoured bite – that last morsel and a sigh of delight – oh what a reward, what an uplifting treat.

Remember to tip the waiter not the windmills. And even if you were the chef, send on your compliments.

Exercise – the recipe for success:

This can be one to add to the journal or just enjoy the adventure of doing. So what is your favourite meal or most perfect snack? I want you to think of something that even the thinking of sparks joy and even a little awe.

Is it an ice cream sundae, a chocolate cake, a big plate of chips, a bowl of colcannon, a vegetable korma or a sturdy stew? Think of it as what would be your first meal after a hostage or desert island rescue – or just one that always pulls you out of the doldrums. That's it, I know you can see it in your mind's eye and probably even taste it this second.

Now I want you to learn how to make it. You can go to the local library and trawl the cookbooks; you can go online and watch a tutorial. You don't have to make it today. But learn the knowhow now and you will have the perfect recipe for when sorrows need easing.

If it was a simple baked potato, explore the range of techniques and the options for toppings. If it was a five-star gourmet speciality then good luck with it but go for it. If it was just a simple slice of bread with butter – discover how to make the bread and how to make the butter. You know, make a meal of it. Learning is fulfilling and knowledge is power. There is not just neuroplasticity here, there is the comfort and reward of achievement.

Éiste le fuaim na habhann agus gheobhaidh tú breac

Listen to the sound of the river and you will get a trout

This is another one of those *seanfhocail* that espouse how patience pays dividends – but it also speaks of how when we attune to our environment and engage our senses, we get such reward. Now maybe it was originally about how to catch your supper, but I hear in it the wisdom of being present, of using the senses in pursuit of a goal, of attuning to the environment, of participating with real perception. To me, it is a prompt to consciously listen.

Conscious listening is not just hearing sounds but listening to them, experiencing their full reality in the moment and presence of your full and true reality. It is listening with original mind to original mind. Listening to a sound is an active meditation, it delivers the observational experience of mindfulness in very immediate terms. Just think of all those wakas and Zen nuggets about 'seeing with our ears'. It doesn't have to all be sweetly babbling brooks either, even the unpleasant sounds can be fished.

Ok if we are to be mindful in our listening or hearing, then the way is to hear the sound, experience the sound non-judgmentally and in listening with focus, take it in, acknowledge its reality and in that moment share our reality with it. And yes that is easy with birdsong and rustling trees but not so much with crying babies or the loud-mouth neighbour – but hearing the 'now reality' of their distress or need to be noticed, can allow loving compassion.

Some days the stream is pleasant music that lands

gratitude, peace or awe. Some days it is a torrent and torment but there are still fish in it – perhaps the loving compassion trout, perhaps the gratitude that you don't live with that neighbour only near them. Some days we may want to actively seek out the pleasant sounds and it is good to seek that joy, that's a fine trout to bring home.

Exercise – hear the room:

Even the hum of the refrigerator or the sounds of traffic can enliven, if listened to rather than just heard. They may not seem to be awe-inspiring sounds but they provide an opportunity to become conscious, present and alert to what is occurring right now. The focus is clarity. The clarity is pureness of the moment. Yes, even the hum can be an *Om mani padme hum* (if I can borrow a little joy from my Buddhist brothers and sisters).

You don't have to select a sound, just stop right now and listen. Wherever you are, just stop and listen for one–two minutes to the stream around you. Even in a seemingly silent room there is a flow of sound, the goings on in the space, the outside noises in the distance, no matter how gentle or rapid the flow, there is flow.

Don't judge or analyse the sounds, simply hear them, fully hear them. If thoughts arise let them pass and return to listening – become conscious that you are listening and hearing – this is experiencing the real world. It may be noisy clatter or the subtle sounds that show that silence is not empty but alive.

Éist le fuaim, it may be a soft whirr in the distance, it may be your beating heart. Experience that – experience being alive. That moment is mindful awareness. That is a caught trout.

Exercise – attune to some nature sounds:

You can go download some ocean scape, rainfall with harp or pure bird song and enjoy the delights of practising your conscious listening but what is stopping you getting outside or even just opening the window. Get some of the real stuff this week. Treat yourself.

We may hear the dawn chorus on the way to bed or to work but do we listen to it, tune in and fully experience it? It is not pre-recorded, it is live, happening as it is only in that moment, yesterday's one was different, tomorrow's will be different again. Listen to it at the next opportunity, be in the moment with it, hear its originality, find its rhythms and patterns, let the awe be and be with it.

Ní lugha an fhroig ná máthair an uilc

Evil may spring from the tiniest thing

This old proverb is often translated into English as 'evil may spring from the tiniest thing'. That little thing – *an fhroig*, denoting a flesh worm, tick or mite – may remind one of the bubonic plague and how a global pandemic can start with a miniscule bite. For centuries, rats were blamed on spreading the disease, but it spread faster than rats can scurry and today we know it wasn't so much the rats as the fleas on the rats, in fact it wasn't so much the fleas as the bacterium *Yersinia pestis* that they carried. So yes, the smallest thing can become a big problem.

Psychologically too, a little incident can become exponential and even an existential crisis – losing your job, a health setback or experiencing unrequited love – is big enough to be noticed but the seed of self-doubt, tension or rumination can begin with a disparaging glance from a stranger or a misplaced or misperceived word from a friend. That little biting moment can infect the flow and nuance of moments throughout the day, days or weeks to follow. We may know this all too well; it may be a regular occurrence, but we can often forget that the way to inoculate is to find perspective – to swat the gnat on your neck and not look for the cloud – that's both the collective noun and the gloomy progression.

The snide look, the unkind remark, the little trigger around the next corner – all tiny. You are bigger than that – and I don't mean grow up and suck it up, I mean there is the rest of whatever is left of the twenty-four hours of this

193

day to not be bothered by a split second of it. It's that small. Your actual life is so much bigger. There is a whole lived experience before it, a whole life lived and a good journey to go, to let a moment occupy more time than it deserves. It happened! Next! Sure, it hurts in that flash, every bite or sting will, but don't pick at it until it become infected.

What the line actually says is 'the little thing is no less than the mother of evil' and in that understanding is the reminder that to birth pain is to carry it around for a long time first. There is a bit involved in creating our current mental health status, one could consider rumination as gestation. Don't indulge the little thing, instead savour a bigger joy – that's a sure antidote.

The proverb says that it is 'no less than' so sure it has a gravity, but we can give it or deny it its weight. This is not ignoring a lump that may be a sign of a cancer, it is more a case of not allowing the freckle on your nose to be the 'disfigurement' that keeps you away from living a full and happy life, out in the world and amongst other people and joy. Context is no less than the mother of joy or the parent of pain.

Exercise – be bigger:

Yes, little things can hurt but little things can also be proportionally placed. The way to defeat the depression that makes your life small, the way to overcome the small-minded disparagers in your life, is to be the bigger person. The way to get a full life with no space for drama, distress or negative emotion triggers, is to grow and expand beyond it all.

You can view 'bigger' as a moral stance, to rise above it, to let the little thing remain insignificant in the context of your spiritually better minded and well-being self. There doesn't have to be inflated ego or self-righteousness in that, just your own self, with dignity and resolve, being unaffected by the littler things.

You can view 'bigger' as more dynamic, as more engagement with the wider opportunities of life. You have so much more going on than to let a single raindrop drown your hope of a beautiful day, to let a single low jab comment ruin your week, to let one incident destroy your life.

You have so much more going on, you have your mindfulness and the larger world it opens, your CBT exercises and the recovery they are building, your positive psychology exercises and all the enriched joys of life that they are unfolding, your personal integrity, your hopes and goals for the future, you have the wide extent of your whole life ahead of you. You have all the slings and arrows of your past, well survived and in the past and you continue to be a hero of your own destiny.

Let the belittlers be little, you are so much bigger, let the vagaries of life be miniscule because you are so much bigger. Fill your life with the good and powerful. Be bigger.

Exercise – power stance:

For a time, there was a trend in public speaking and motivational seminars to get prospective go-getters and those unsure of their prowess, to adopt a superhero pose or power stance for a few moments before they had to perform, take the call or write the email or knock the task out the park.

The standing with your hands on your hips or however your favourite superhero adopts their big stance, engendered that childlike awe and fired that sense of 'can do' within the imagination and spirit. It playfully tricked the brain or the nerves, in line – you channelled the power stance and powered on.

The power stance works for the team brief, it can work for little doubts and minor problems. You can adopt the stance right now or whenever you need that extra confidence boost or you can just picture yourself in your head as doing it, or as bigger, stronger more self-assured – it is a visual affirmation.

You can hum a theme tune too, you may want to laugh and sure why not, you have time to laugh because you've got this.

Dein maith i n-aghaidh an uilc

Do good in return for evil

This is not a moral imperative; it is not telling us to be good or obedient; there is no guilt or shame implied here in not adhering to all the tenants of any particular faith or failing to fastidiously stick to the rules every moment of our life. It is bigger than that. It is how to reply to evil – do good, not to atone or be upstanding but to defeat the bad. It is not so much a moral compass as ringside instruction. It's the reminder that you have a powerful uppercut. Its ok to KO the bad.

Sure, it is proper to aspire to be virtuous over malevolent but once in the ring with evil don't be shy in hitting back. No holding, no biting, no below the belt, just your pure sweet punches and your dancing feet. Utilise your well-trained skill, your heart and your winning moves. Dazzle evil with your good. Be undisputed.

It is a better choice not just on a moral/spiritual level but psychological and physically. Staying on the positive path can be hard in the face of assault or intimidation or provocation but why bring more negativity into the world. How I react to saboteurs and malice is I go have a good day, I do something positive with friends or family or for myself – I don't default into revenge or revenge fantasy – I go generate some good instead.

We previously spoke of being bigger. This proverb is also the mindset of being bigger. You don't have to be dragged down to the level of tit for tat. You can change how your mind is set on it. I often reflect on how the expectation upon an injustice or disservice done, was 'an eye for an eye' until Jesus reframed it to how about we try 'do unto others as we would have them do unto us'. If we are all doing the good first there is no opportunity to cause another to seek revenge, there is no avenging on your own behalf. Doing good back to any evil or injustice or disservice or discomfort in your life, is you in with the good, in a good place not stuck in bad. How freeing is that?

It is not that you are going to give the benefit of your time, energy and skill to advance the social standing or pocket of a perpetrator. By now hopefully we have dropped them from our story. They have been forgiven, let go, forgotten about, arraigned or testified against – what every it took to get beyond them. But we can on this other side of our past trauma, move forward with goodness in our heart and goodness in our deeds.

We can move well beyond the evil doer but still combat the evil done. Run a marathon for domestic violence awareness, a rape crisis organisation, a childhood neglect charity. Volunteer or donate at a drop-in centre or food bank.

Or simply do not pass the shit on that was passed on to us. We can hold the line in not letting our own family's inter-generational trauma reach the next generation. In being good examples. In being our good, not damaged, selves.

Action. Three for one:

The ask here is to meet evil three for one. The evil in our

life may be our own self-perception or self-esteem so what three positive things can we do this week to tilt things in our own favour – radical acceptance, reframing, positive affirmations. The evil in our world may be the evils of the world, poverty, injustice, wars, etc. What three good things can you do to win a round – sponsor a child in poverty, join a peace movement, register to vote? The evil in our world may be our personal circumstance; what moves are needed here – what comes to mind?

'Chonaic mé cheana thú', arsa an cat leis an mbainne beirithe

'I saw you before', said the cat to the boiling milk

This evocative *seanfhocal* warns us to beware of the same mistakes. It is not so much 'once bitten twice shy' and so a prompt to be vigilantly fearful. No, it is more a reminder to recognise the harmful potential as you meet it. You don't have to shy away from the dangers or unpleasant parts of life, just know that they exist. Recognise and be aware.

Ok so we can learn a life lesson from our mistakes, but we don't need to repeat them like the times tables to actually learn from them. Too often we wander into the same territory over and over; similar relationships, same self-doubts, same misplaced trust or worse – hope of different outcome this time round. Scalding milk will always scald. Risky behaviour always puts you at risk. Embracing rumination or anticipatory worry always grips you back. Recognise and be aware.

Mindful practices are all about learning to recognise – to comprehend, to see – the reality. Mindfulness is to observe and to be fully present to the now. It is easier to not slip into automatically sipping the boiling milk if you are fully present and awake to the world around you. The word 'recognise' comes from the Latin *recognoscere* 'to know again' – to comprehend the familiar or the past experience. *Cognoscere* is actually to 'learn' as much as to 'know'. So, yes we can learn from our past, we can learn to identify the good and the bad, to see the potential and the reality of the moment before us or the moment we are in. We can therefore not just recognise but respond accordingly.

To be alert to danger is good, to live in fear of it is not so healthy. Seeing the reality is not just positioning oneself to not get scalded, it is not having to occupy the rest of your life with regret or hyper-vigilant anticipation of the next mistake. Sure, that inbuilt negative bias that all humans have, that's the cat and the boiling milk, that's all the previous red flags proudly fluttering but this proverb echoes that 'here we go again' recognition – the realisation that comes in time to avert the catastrophe. The boiled milk that scalded before is enough of an experience – no need for repeats.

That said it does not close you down to looking at the pot and the simmering milk – you know its potential – you are aware of its nature; you can respond to the situation now with clarity – cognisant of the reality of the situation. You can recognise it for what it is. You can adjust your trajectory. You have seen it before; you know the score. You are seeing it now; you can change the outcome. You don't have to tip it on to yourself. You don't have to lap it up. You can give it a miss. You can even turn the heat off.

We don't have to make the same mistakes every time. No matter the mistake, no matter the repeat behaviour, we can learn to not continue to do it – in the moment, we can choose another option – we can be different now. Being here and now, mindful in both the sense of being present and in the sense of intellectual perception is how we know again, how we recognise and pre-empt the mistake – but also how we recognise our true self.

Exercise – mirror, mirror:

Mirror affirmations are popular in many positive psychology circles because you are not 'shying away', you are looking yourself in the eye – you are directly speaking to yourself. The process helps imprint strong positive sentiments. It is not a confrontation, not a harsh look at your failings, there is no inner critic here. It is the recognition of yourself and a commitment affirmation to yourself. You will make a positive commitment towards the end of it – to be more resilient or to enjoy life more or forgive or love or be grateful. Your brain and spirit will recognise the sincerity of it, you will communicate it to your soul, incorporate it and live it.

Simply look in a mirror, look at yourself. No judgement here on how you look, no wishing you were younger or whatever, you are just noticing your reflection in that mirror. Let any discomfort go. Now really look – recognise – relearn your face; notice the shape of your mouth, the breath in your nostrils, your searching eyes, all your familiar features, your humanity – look at yourself, see yourself.

Now take a moment to know that you are more than the face looking back at you – you are the physical self; become aware of your corporal body, your solid self, this person will hear your commitment, this person will absorb it, this person will live it. Make your commitment, say it out to yourself. Whatever it is you need to hear and in hearing record it deep. It may be, if this proverb has struck a chord, that from now on you will be mindful to the dangers of neglect and conceit, be alert to the triumphs and the compassionate responses. It is what you need most to hear – it may be 'good job so far', 'stick with it' or even 'you got this'.

Still aware of your physical self, take one last look in that mirror – recognise – this person has heard it, this person has absorbed it, this person will live it.

Dá fhaid é an lá, tagann an oíche

However long the day, night comes

We all get bad days, too tired, too under the weather, too agitated or under too much pressure to be able to function with full mindfulness or even enough energy to get through the cornflakes, never mind skip and whistle through the day. We just need to accept that we cannot be at our best 24/7 – and that's ok – one bad day doesn't have to become a new depression or anxious episode. We can recognise it for what it is. We can take it in our stride. It's one long day, it is not the rest of our life.

Having a bad day is not a let off from doing the right thing either, it is not a starting gun to run yourself down, it is not an excuse to slip back or hit the default mode – we can continue to endeavour to be the good and positive in the world. It's a moment. You are not bound to it. You can regain composure and move on. Whatever the trials and consternations – there is still an evening to come. And it comes.

Hard days can be set aside. Dropped, not perpetuated. Evenings can be enjoyed. Evenings can be mindful and harmonious recuperations from the long day. Mindfulness can replenish you after a long day. The pessimists say all good things must come to an end, well this positive injection to the negative says that all bad things must come to an end too – depression, fatigue, anxiety, slow progress, even long days.

There is an African proverb that comes at it from the other side – 'however long the night, morning comes'. So, if it's a long dark night of the soul, then know, light is on its way.

Action. Have a bath:

At the end of a long day nothing is as soothing as a bath – some balneotherapy, some *sanitas per aquas* (health through water), some simple 'soak and relax' time. For many there is a womblike experience available via a simple bath, the posture, the warm comfort of the water, the held 'suspension within the fluid' that provides a psychological relief to tensions and the angst of the day. Physiologically, relaxing in water can reduce physical pain and inflammation, calm the nervous system and alter the production and release of hormones and stress chemicals including serotonin, beta-endorphin and cortisol.

If you are trying to be more conscientious with water usage, you don't have to fill the bath to get some of the benefits, you can just sit in an unfilled bath. The posture we adopt in a bath, horizontal but supported, provides a sensation of security and elicits relaxation. So have a dry bath, get in and just chill out for fifteen minutes, by all means from time to time read this book in it.

Of course, you may want to try a sound bath – to savour and bathe in a beautiful piece of music or a set of recorded sounds from nature or recordings of mantras or chants be it Gregorian or Buddhist, it is the immersion in the sound, the surrendering of tensions, the letting your woes be washed away.

You may want to try a forest bathing (shinrin yoku) which has an amazing impact upon lowering cortisol and blood pressure, but if your long day ends in night-time, a trek through the woods is not always practicable but you can bring the forest indoors, you can populate your home or a single room with houseplants and equally benefit from the observing, relishing and tranquil surrender to the good in that greenery.

Is fearr muinighin mhaith ná droch-aigneadh

Favour good hope over bad intention

This is more of a recommendation than a commandment – but you could interoperate it is a moral imperative. You could adopt it as a personal commandment. Favouring good intentions, choosing to see the positive and go with it, over and above the call or default of bad intention is a good thing. A very good thing. A life-changing thing. A way to break from the grip of misery and negativity, a way beyond your current woes or lifelong setbacks.

This proverb is all about positive vibrations. It is all about negating negative vibrations. What you put into the world you might just get back – be that a 'garbage in, garbage out' or a 'good karma' perspective. We know all too well that misery breeds misery – there is a spiral down – in part because that negative bias is heightened in our sorrow or distress and it is also that we tend to steer clear or be swept clear of positive opportunities when miserable; we are less likely to venture out or partake when not feeling so great – but it might just be what we need to reverse the downward turn.

Many of this book's proverbs prompt this mindset but it really is the key to overcoming doom and gloom, to be your own ray of sunshine or at least a torch-bearer for your aspiration to live a good, non-depressed, non-agitated, better life. In doing good or participating in positive actions and good social interaction, you flood your brain and body with positive endorphins. In the act of the good deed or hopeful moment, it not only gave you an 'in the moment' sense of well-being but the more positive experiences we achieve/encounter, the more they arise – we switch on our positivity bias. Good hope fosters more hope but good hope quells bad intention too. These acts of good hope or expressions of goodwill are the spiral up. Doing a good turn is the upward turn.

Maybe the good turn is toward yourself – to stop punishing yourself, to get up and go do something nice, to just take a step into the better side of life. Maybe the good is toward your family, friends, community. It's all about disarming the bad intentions (the stifling scenario) of your current psychological woes with the good emotions of better intentions of doing more hopeful things.

This book is nearing its end. It doesn't mean the good in it that you have found must end, carry it on, keep it with you and extend it in to the universe and the world around you. Be the good hope, become your good intentions.

Actions. Will the good and bring good will:

Some of these you will have done from previous exercises, they don't have to be one off events, they can become how you express your loving kindness, your positive motivations, your active participation with the world, your source of inspiration and joy. Do them often, add more to the list.

- ❖ Do a good turn for a neighbour or friend.
- ❖ Have a clear out and donate to the local charity shop – not the rubbish but the usable stuff that you don't use often.
- ❖ Do a charity run for a favourite charity.
- ❖ Lobby or organise for a good cause or community event.
- ❖ Volunteer.

- ❖ Support.
- ❖ Listen.
- ❖ Commune.
- ❖ Be kind of heart and spirit.
- ❖ Show others how to survive and thrive.
- ❖ Be your own full potential.

Tuar an t-ádh agus tiocfaidh sé

Predict good fortune and it will come

This proverb is the antidote to brooding and rumination, it is the invitation to ponder the positive. It is not about fantasising a better outcome – although we can engage in a little of that through visualisation, to acclimatise ourselves to the potential of experiencing all the joys life has to offer – it is more about making good luck happen, about manifesting your brighter destiny. How? – by simply predicting it. Instead of occupying your time with delving into the negative past or the fret of the future 'what ifs' – why not anticipate a stronger, more empowered self, one free to love, laugh and embrace life.

The proverb is about envisioning the better – indeed expecting and beckoning the better. It is about readjusting your mindset to the power of positivity. Too often we can set our expectations too low, too often being low leaves us bereft of any good expectation at all and so this switch to 'the good on its way' is a good practice to engage in, to reset the mind and spirit towards reception of the good when it comes.

It is not about hope, it is about accepting that you deserve better and can achieve or receive better. Better is out there to be had, by stepping out of the rumination and the habitual replaying of the negative narratives, you can shape a happier tale. You can elevate your awareness of the positive, you can move in the flow of the goodness of experiences and encounters, you can enjoy the world around you.

Yes, we have been actively engaged in actions and exercise all through this book, to bring on the good or find the positive. To have the good and positive circuit-break our angst, apprehension and depression. The repeat is the conditioning, the repeat hunting of the good is good hunting. Do more of it. It doesn't only have to be to stop a depression or intervene with an episode, it can be the life you live every day. All the good days to come.

This proverb is about taking that mindset and aspiration beyond the day you finish the book. It is about a future of more genuine joy and authentic happiness; it is about being unruffled or more controlled from here on in. It is the reward of good fortune you deserve. Predict it, envisage it, expect it – and it will come – there is surety in that.

Action. Envisage the good:

Fortune or fate may just be a self-fulfilling prophecy, what you expect you might just manifest or at the very least not notice the other events of the day or week that counter the argument. The proverb reminds us to 'start as you mean to go on'. The ask here is to start as you want to go on. First thing every morning meet the day with positive regards and positive expectation. It might just be a good day, don't stand in its way with worry or lack of hope.

If you wake up thinking this is going to be a terrible day, you are setting your brain to scan for all the negative things, you collate the information to make the day appear terrible. So it ends up that you are still dwelling so much on the burnt toast that you fail to hear the birdsong, fail to register the smile of a passer-by, fail to notice the sun is shining, fail to put your hand out for the bus – now you are late – it's a terrible day.

But you enabled it. Had you been mindful and not mind full of burnt toast and 'poor me' and 'what a shitty day', the bird song might have lifted your mood, the smile may cause you to smile back, breaking self-pity or rumination for a few seconds, enough to look up and notice a better day forming and then with your head up you would have seen your bus approaching. This does not mean you deserved it, you simply walked into it, sleep-walked into it – did not awaken to other possibilities and better outcomes.

If you wake up thinking this is a great day, the toast may still burn but it is a very minor setback not an arrow through the heart and maybe it's an opportunity to leave early and grab a bagel on the way to your destination. If you're not under pressure to be anywhere, have a nice stroll to a pleasant café for a breakfast treat – soak up a little warmth from the sun and share a smile or two – already the day is getting better, fulfilling its destiny to be great.

Fortune can be about choices. It is how you see the world, how you choose to react or respond to it. Today – right now – why not envisage the good. Why not have a great one?

Caitheann síor-shileadh an chlioch

Continuous weathering wears the rock

We all have rocks on our path, some of us have mountains in our way, the secret is to get the right footwear. In reading this book and following the exercises and actions you have trained for terrain. Practising mindfulness and positive psychology techniques is equipping yourself for the terrain and building stamina for the trek. By now your thoughts and life circumstances should not be throwing up such high mountains or earth-quaking gorges in your path but the road can still be rocky and winding some days and even if not as demanding as before, the journey – trek or stroll – always requires energy and vigilance.

I featured this proverb in a previous book (*By Time is Everything Revealed*) in the context of sticking with mindfulness practices, to deliver mastery of mindfulness, and certainly this proverb is a reminder that constancy and diligence can erode the most momentous of tasks, ease the difficult asks. The more you practise the more you achieve; it can take time but the mind-wandering gets less, the capability for self-control increases. The obstacles will erode.

I am reminded of Isaiah 40:4 'Every valley *shall* be raised up, every mountain and hill made low; the rough ground shall become level, the rugged places a plain'. In the meantime, keep on keeping on – and if you can add to that a line from that Curtis Mayfield song then … 'Continue to give, continue to live for what you know is right'.

Take it all in your stride.

Action. Be continuous:

Be continuous, keep going, keep living, keep dreaming, keep the faith, survive every episode and thrive in the times between, laugh and love as much as you can, take delight from life and comfort from the good things. You will wear down those obstacles in your path – the path will get smoother. A pathway is made by walking on it. Be brave and be tough, all the pain has been useful. You continue to persevere. You will persevere.

Now go weather the hell out of those rocks.

LIST OF PROVERBS

1. Teas gréine is gar do dhubhadh – Sunshine follows gloom.

2. An té ná gabhann cómhairle gabhadh sé cómhrac – Whoever will not accept advice must accept strife.

3. Gnáthamh na hoibre an t-eolas – Knowledge comes through practice.

4. Gáire maith agus codladh fada, an dá leigheas is fearr i leabhar an dochtúra – A good laugh and a long sleep, the two best cures in the doctor's book.

5. Fearr déanaighe ná ró-dhéanaighe – Better late than never.

6. An té nach bhfuil láidir ní folair dó a bheith glic. Who is not strong must be clever.

7. Cuinnibh an cnámh is leanfaidh an madra thu – Keep hold of the bone and the dog will follow you.

8. Caora mhór an t-uan i bhfad – A lamb becomes a sheep if you carry it long enough.

9. Ná beannaigh don diabhal go mbeannaí sé duit –Don't greet the devil until he greets you.

10. Bíonn dhá insint ar scéal agus dhá leagan déag ar amhrán. There are two versions to a story and twelve arrangements to a song.

11. I ndiaidh a chéile a thógtar na caisleáin – Castles are built one after the other.

12. Is minic a ghearr duine slat a bhuail a dhroim féin – A man often cut a stick which beat his own back.

13. Leigheas gach brón comhrádh – Conversation is a cure for every sorrow.

14. An té nach trua leis do chás, ná déan do ghearán leis – He who does not sympathise with your plight, don't make your complaint to him.

15. An rud is measa le duine ar domhan n'fheadair sé nach é lár a leasa é – The very thing a person dreads most in the world could

be the best thing for him.

16. Léig an donas chun deiridh, a n-dúil s' nach d-tiocaidh se choidche – Leave the bad luck to the last, in hopes that it may never come.

17. Is leithide an bualtach satail ann – Trampling on dung only spreads it more.

18. Ní dhéanfaidh smaoineamh an treabhadh duit – You'll never plough a field by turning it over in your mind.

19. Ná biodh do theangaidh fa do chrios – Do not keep your tongue under your belt.

20. Doras feasa fiafraí – The door to wisdom is asking.

21. Is doimhin é poll an amhrais – Deep is the hole of doubt.

22. Is ceirín do gach uile chréacht an fhoighde – Patience is a plaster for all sores.

23. Níl leigheas ar an gcathú ach é a mharú le foighne – There's no cure for regret except to kill it with patience.

24. Ná tabhair thú féin suas don bhrón agus ná bí do do chiapadh féin d'aonghnó – Do not give in to sadness, torment not yourself with brooding.

25. Ní bhíonn an rath ach mara mbíonn an smacht – There is only success where there is discipline.

26. Tá lán mara eile ins an fhairge – There is another tide in the sea.

27. An rud a ghoilleas ar an gcroí caithfidh an t-súil é a shileas – What pains the heart must be washed away with tears.

28. An rud a líonas an tsúil líoann sé an croí – What fills the eye fills the heart.

29. Ar uairibh thigid na hanacraí, is fearr san ná a dteacht an éinfheacht – It is well that misfortunes come but from time to time and not altogether.

30. Ní hé lá na gaoithe lá na scolb – The windy day is not the day for thatching.

31. Is maith an cúnamh an lá breá – A fine day is a help to everyone.

32. Is feárr an mhaith atá ná an dá mhaith a bhí – Better the good

thing that is than two good things that were.

33. Níl íseal ná uasal ach thíos seal agus thuas seal – There is neither low nor high but down for a while and up for a while.

34. Is fearr an té a éiríonn ná an té a thiteas – Better the person who gets up to try again than the one who falls (and stays there).

35. Is maith le Dia féin cúnamh – Even God himself likes help.

36. Gach aon ní mar is cóir – is an pota ar an driosúr! – Everything as it should be – and the pot on the dresser!

37. Ní haon mhaith a bheith ag caoineadh nuair a imíonn an tsochraid – There's no good in keening when the funeral has moved off.

38. Chun 'uil tuile ó mheud nach d-traoghann – However great the flood, it will ebb.

39. Is éascaí nóin ná maidin - Evening is speedier than morning.

40. Nuair a bhíonn an fíon istigh, bíonn an ciall amuigh – When the wine is in, sense is out.

41. Is fearr rith maith ná droch-sheasamh – A good run is better than a bad stand.

42. Is fearr leath-bhuilín ná a bheith gan arán – Half a loaf is better than to be without any bread.

43. *Ní troimide an chaora a holann* – The sheep does not mind the weight of the wool.

44. Is minic a mhaolaigh béile maith brón – It is often a good meal eased sorrow.

45. Éist le fuaim na habhann agus gheobhaidh tú breac – Listen to the sound of the river and you will get a trout.

46. Ní lugha an fhroig ná máthair an uilc – Evil may spring from the tiniest thing.

47. Dein maith i n-aghaidh an uilc – Do good in return for evil.

48. 'Chonaic mé cheana thú', arsa an cat leis an mbainne beirithe – 'I saw you before', said the cat to the boiling milk.

49. Dá fhaid é an lá, tagann an oíche. However long the day, night comes

50. Is fearr muinighin mhaith ná droch-aigneadh – Favour good hope over bad intention.

51. Tuar an t-ádh agus tiocfaidh sé – Predict good fortune and it will come.

52. Caitheann síor-shileadh an chlioch – Continuous weathering wears the rock.

BIBLIOGRAPHY

Affleck, G. & Tennen, H. (1996). 'Construing benefits from adversity: Adaptational significance and dispositional underpinnings'. *Journal of Personality, 64*, 899–922.

Beck, A.T. (1967). *Depression: Causes and treatment.* Philadelphia: University of Pennsylvania Press.

Beck, A.T. (1976). *Cognitive therapy and the emotional disorders.* New York: International Universities Press.

Bryant, F. & Veroff, J. (2007). *Savoring: A new model of positive experience.* Mahwah, NJ: Lawrence Erlbaum Associates.

Csíkszentmihályi, M. (1996). *Flow and the psychology of discovery and invention.* New York: Harper Collins.

Dobson, K. S., & Block, L. (1988). *Historical and philosophical bases of cognitive behavioural theories. Handbook of Cognitive behavioural Therapies.* UK: Guilford Press.

Ellis, A. (1962). *Reason and Emotion in Psychotherapy.* New York: Stuart.

Fredrickson, B.L., & Joiner, T. (2002). 'Positive emotions trigger upward spirals toward emotional well-being'. *Psychological Science, 13*, 172–175.

Gaffney, M. (2011). *Flourishing – how to achieve a deeper sense of well-being, meaning and purpose even when facing adversity.* UK: Penguin Books.

Green R., & Turner G. (2010). Growing evidence for the influence of meditation on brain and behaviour. *Neuropsychol. Rehabil.* 20, 306–311

Hayes, S.C., *et al.* (1999). *Acceptance and commitment therapy.* New York: Guilford Press.

Kabat-Zinn, J. (1990). *Full catastrophe living: Using the wisdom of your body and mind to face stress, pain and illness.* New York: Delacorte.

Leary, M.R., *et al.* (2007). 'Self-compassion and reactions to unpleasant self-relevant events: the implications of treating oneself kindly'. *Journal of Personality and Social Psychology, 92,* 887–904.

LeDoux JE. (1996*). The Emotional Brain.* New York: Simon and Schuster.

LeDoux JE. (2002). *Synaptic Self: How Our Brains Become Who We Are.* New York: Viking.

Lindsay EK. *et al.,* (2018) 'Acceptance lowers stress reactivity: Dismantling mindfulness training in a randomized controlled trial'. *Psychoneuroendocrinology.* 87: 63–73.

Linley, P. A. & Joseph, S. (Eds.). (2004) *Positive psychology in practice.* Hoboken, John Wiley & Sons, Inc.

Marks I. (1987). *Fears, Phobias, and Rituals: Panic, Anxiety and Their Disorders.* New York: Oxford Univ. Press.

O'Morain, P. (2023). *Acceptance: Create Change and Move Forward.* UK: Hodder & Stoughton.

Peterson, C & Seligman, M (2004). Character strengths and virtues: A handbook and classification. Oxford: Oxford University Press.

Rubia K. (2009). 'The neurobiology of meditation and its clinical effectiveness in psychiatric disorders'. *Biol. Psychol.* 82, 1–1110. 1016

Seligman, M. (1991). *Learned optimism.* New York: Knopf.

Sin, NL & Lyubomirsky, S. (2009) 'Enhancing Well-Being and Alleviating Depressive Symptoms with Positive Psychology Interventions: A Practice-Friendly Meta-Analysis'. *Journal of clinical psychology.* Vol. 65(5), 467–487

Watkins, E.R. (2016). *Rumination-focused cognitive-behavioral therapy for depression*. New York: Guilford.

Wood, A.M., *et al.* (2008). 'The role of gratitude in the development of social support, stress, and depression: Two longitudinal studies'. *Journal of Research in Personality*, 42, 854–871.

52 PROVERBS
To Build Resilience Against Anxiety and Panic

Fiann Ó Nualláin

Fiann Ó Nuallain brings the ancient wisdom of Irish proverbs to life with the help of modern techniques like mindfulness, positive psychology and cognitive behavioural therapy. In this practical self-help book, you'll find 52 proverbs that speak directly to the worries and stresses of modern life.

These proverbs are more than clever idioms. They are the accumulated wisdom of our ancestors passed down through generations as a way to navigate life's challenges. By reading these proverbs and following the accompanying exercises, you'll be able to chart a course through life's obstacles and find greater happiness, calm and meaning.

So if you're struggling with anxiety or just looking for practical guidance for living a more fulfilling life, *52 Proverbs to Build Resilience against Anxiety and Panic* is the perfect resource. With its blend of ancient wisdom and modern techniques, it's sure to become a go-to self-help book for anyone seeking peace and calm in a hectic world.

The Holistic Gardner: First Aid from the Garden
Fiann Ó Nualláin

A handy guide to quick and effective natural first-aid treatments for commonly occurring accidents and complaints, derived from garden and kitchen sources.

From a thorn prick to heatstroke, from chapped hands to hay fever, from pesticide poisoning to wasp stings: all of these can be treated on site with what you grow. The plant beside you as you work or relax in the garden can be the answer to the hive, ache or watery eye.

Written by a professional gardener with a lifetime's experience of accidents that can happen in the garden, all the information you need on first response, the essential plants and homemade remedy preparation is combined in this book.

The Holistic Gardner: Natural Cures for Common Ailments
Fiann Ó Nualláin

The must-have guide to natural remedies for common ailments. Use items from your garden and store-cupboard for complaints ranging from coughs and colds to aches and pains that allows you to save money and avoid taking mass-produced chemicals on a regular basis. Fiann gives simple step-by-step instructions to make straightforward salves and ointments, teas, rinses and syrups that will fill the first-aid cupboard, as well as identifying plants that can be used straight away with no preparation required.

Fiann's singular knowledge of the properties and uses of herbs, fruit and flowers from the garden makes fascinating reading, as well as having extensive practical applications.

www.mercierpress.ie